WHAT'S
MOST
IMPORTANT?

WHAT'S MOST IMPORTANT?

PRIORITIES FOR LIVING AN INTELLIGENT LIFE

DR. WILLIAM S. SVOBODA

Table of Contents

Introduction 11

A Short History of the Research 13

Factor 1 *Gaining and Maintaining Physical Health* 21

Natural Foods 24

Variety 25

Moderation 26

Preparation Ideas 28

Some Additional Ideas about Nutrition.................... 30

EXERCISE 34

Your Body—Use It or Lose It—A Case for
Variety and Moderation in Physical Exercise 34

Factor 2 *Gaining and Maintaining Mental Health* 47

What You Think About Tends to Come About 50

Mental Health and Stress 51

Some Stress Basics: 51

It's natural to have stress. 51

Mental Health Strategies to Prevent,
Reduce, Control and Use Stress 54

Mind as Tool 68

Factor 3 *Gaining and Maintaining Financial Security* ... 71

Behaviors of People Who Are Gaining and
Maintaining Wealth 73

Step 1: Live Below Your Means 75

Step 2: Start a Savings Plan—Pay Your
Future First and Then Live on the Rest 77

Step 3: Create an Emergency or Crisis Fund 79

Step 4: Do You Need Insurance? 80

Step 5: If You Have to Buy Something on
Credit, You Can't Afford It...................................... 81

Step 6: Learn to Delay Gratification......................... 84

Step 7: Think About Your Retirement 86

Factor 4   ***Mastering and Using Problem-Solving and Critical-Thinking Skills*** 95

  The Importance of Words 96

  All History Is Interpretation......................101

  Three Ways of Observing and Reporting Data 102

  Basic Decision-Making Steps 104

  The Best Approach to Solving Problems Is Preventing Them......................................106

  Knowing the Difference between Form and Substance 107

  Using the Scientific Method......................110

  Human Consequences of Decision-Making Matrix 112

  Some Final Thoughts about Decision-Making Tradeoffs 116

  Sunk Costs...117

  Make Lists and Prioritize...........................118

  Concentrate on Things You Can Influence..............120

Factor 5   ***Acting Responsibly to Others, the Environment, and Yourself***..............................125

  Using Basic Ethics as a Basis for Explaining Responsibilities 126

  What Is Acting Responsibly? 128

  Responsibility to Others 130

  Responsibility to the Environment..........................133

  What Can You and I Do?.............................135

  Responsibility to Yourself...........................141

  Final Thoughts...150

Living Intelligently: A Final Note and a Challenge..........155

WHAT'S MOST IMPORTANT?

Introduction

Let's start a revolution. I want us to start a revolution. *We need to start a revolution.* I don't mean an armed rebellion against the government or other forms of authority. I mean an intellectual and behavioral revolution that questions the status quo at every level and then makes changes based on that which we deliberately determine to be most important. Decades of research have led me to the conclusion that most of us are squandering our lives because we take so much for granted. Further, we can make our lives—and the lives of those around us—much more meaningful and prosperous if we take some time to think about what we are doing and why we are doing it.

I suggest that the first step in this process is asking the question that is the title of this book: *What's Most Important?* Very few of the people with whom I have spoken and worked have even considered this question. When I answered this question for myself and applied it to my life, I was surprised at how the answers seemed to fall into place and how profoundly they would change my thinking and, more importantly, my behaviors. I found the same appropriateness and applicability when I considered what's most important to groups and organizations from families to national governments. If you generally agree with the importance of the five factors I will present, then you too might want to adjust your thinking and behaviors. The following might be some shifts in your life that could result:

- A shift in using your discretionary time from seeking entertainment to seeking more information you can use to improve your life and the lives of those around you.

- A shift from unquestioningly following others (authority figures, books, organizations, governments, and so on) to a healthy skepticism and critical analysis of the ideas and actions they espouse.

11

- A shift from blind acceptance of traditional school subjects to reasoned, carefully chosen, useful-in-life subjects in all schools, kindergarten through graduate school.

- A shift from today's sports-based, combative, win-lose mentality in decision-making and negotiating to a problem-solving process based on win-win solutions that emphasize positive human consequences.

- A shift from the standard American lifestyle that emphasizes junk food and being sedentary to a lifestyle that emphasizes plant-based, nutritious "real foods" and a variety of physical exercise.

- A shift from the focus on unlimited exploitation of nature's resources to the increased utilization of human mental resources to conserve and nurture what nature has given us.

- A shift generally from bigger to smaller.

- A shift from our seeking happiness through consumption to seeking happiness through adding value to others, to the environment, and to ourselves.

There are many more shifts in thoughts and behaviors that will be discussed and advocated in this book, but the ideas above are representative of changes I will be asking you to consider.

Note that I am not asking you to accept my suggestions without scrutiny or critical analysis or without anticipating the consequences of applying them to your life. I am asking you to carefully consider each idea and decide whether you (1) accept it, (2) reject it, or (3) can modify it to make it better.

A Short History of the Research

For several decades the fundamental research question that I have pursued as a professional educator, philosopher, parent, and member of the human race has been, What's worth knowing? Throughout grade school, high school, undergraduate work, and graduate study, I was aware that most of what I was "learning" was not applicable to my life as I knew it. Nor was it applicable to others' lives as I observed them. On the few occasions when I summoned up the courage and expressed my doubts about the usefulness of a subject, my teachers justified it as important for an upcoming test or as necessary background information so I could understand future classes. This meant that I was spending years and years in school learning this stuff so I could progress further in school. Nobody seemed to be worrying about what I should know *after* school. No one seemed to have ever thought about how, or even whether, what they were teaching me could be used in some constructive way to improve my life, society, or the environment.

As a public school teacher, I questioned the value of most of what I was asked to teach. But times were different then, and a teacher could adjust the curriculum to fit student interests and probable needs. Within limits, I could ignore what was boring and useless, and teach content and skills that students could relate to as they were being taught. For example, when my middle school syllabus told me I should have my class of gifted students studying rocks and minerals, a student's question about the Cold War led to the class researching why the Soviet people did not spontaneously rebel against the Communist regime, overthrow it, and live happily ever after like we do in the United States.

As the students did academic research on the topic, I secretly organized my class as a Communist cell. I individually and secretly told each of four students they were my spies and I wanted each of them to tell me of any negative things said about my class, the school or me. Each student thought he was my only spy. I further told each of my "spies" to especially watch three students. These were my other three informers. A few days later I had the four spies report their findings to me and the class. I confronted all the "guilty" students with their crimes against my regime. Perhaps the biggest surprises occurred when the informers realized they were especially being watched. My students then vividly understood how spying and mistrust among neighbors in a cell system of suppression would not allow any rebellion among the Soviet people. They had experienced, at least momentarily, how helpless they would feel living in a system laden with informers. They also understood that this same practice could be used anywhere. They learned something valuable that they could use right now. This kind of freedom to teach the relevant was the beginning of my personal revolution and my more formal pursuit of what is worth knowing.

My doctorate emphasized curriculum development, but the graduate classes I took did not critically analyze what was being taught in the schools. The emphasis was always on *how we could teach better,* not on *what would be better to teach.* The curriculum was and still is going largely unchallenged and unanalyzed. As a professor, I was disillusioned to discover that the state, regional, and national professional organizations for curriculum development did not have curriculum or subject analysis as even a minor goal, let alone as the major goal. It seemed so obvious—and still does—that the first thing any school system should do is analyze what needed to be taught. What was most important to teach? I was discouraged and almost quit professional education.

After some reflection, however, I determined that I would quietly do what I thought curriculum developers should be doing: *I would do my own private research to discover what is worth knowing.* I must say that it has been a long but very exciting and interesting quest. I presently have files full of data that I have found to be directly applicable to the human enterprise. The data are generally applicable across social, political, religious, and educational divisions and all the other divisions we could divide ourselves into. It is useful information. It is practical knowledge. It is knowledge that I have personally tested and used to gain personal success in many different ways. I know it works because it has worked for me. The most astounding thing I learned, however, is that nearly all of what I discovered to be worth knowing was *not* taught to me in the twenty or so years I spent as a student in formal education. When I share some of the practical data I have collected, the most frequent comment is "Why didn't my school or parents teach me this when I was young? My life would have been so much easier and better."

As I gathered my findings of concepts, ideas, skills, and other useful information, I had some opportunities to subversively sneak them into the university. Of course, I would slip them into my classes when possible. I would include them in professional papers I would write or edit. I would include them in conference presentations.

My best formal chance to use them came when one of the professors at my university, who was an author of the famous (or infamous depending on how you saw it) Dick and Jane reading series, recommended me as a coauthor for a civics textbook another professor was rewriting. I convinced my coauthor that I should write some chapters on skills that a good citizen should possess to be an active and positive participant in government and in society. I wrote sections on basic semantics, precise use of words, decision-making, the scientific method, problem-solving, propaganda analysis, and recognizing logical fallacies. At the time this edition of *The Missouri Citizen* was published, no other citizenship or government text in the United State dealt with these skills. I was proud of that breakthrough. As far as I can tell, to this day no other middle or high school civics text includes that kind of data.

As my useful information files grew, I determined that I needed to do something to make the information more widely available. I decided that I would write several short, individual chapters about concepts or skills I had researched and found especially useful in my life. I determined that I would write them at the rate of one chapter per week for a year. At the end of the year I started submitting my concept papers to publishers. Finally, I was able to publish *Your Choices, Your Life*, which is a book about gaining increased control of your life. A second edition is now available.

After retiring from the university to pursue my research full time, I found myself as a willing caregiver for my father and then my wife. This was my primary occupation for about a decade. I was able to continue my research during this time but wasn't able to pursue the dissemination of my findings. When I was finally able to spend sustained time thinking about how to disseminate all my data, I realized that I needed to organize the data into a structure people could identify with. My organizing question became "What's most important?" In other words, what are the needs, issues, desires, problems, and concerns that are most important in the lives of human beings? That's what the rest of this book is about.

At this time in the development of my research, I submit to you that the following five factors compose a reasonable basis for answering the question, "What's most important?" The five factors are:

- Gaining and Maintaining Physical Health.

- Gaining and Maintaining Mental Health.

- Gaining and Maintaining Financial Security.

- Mastering and Using Problem-Solving and Critical-Thinking Skills.

- Acting Responsibly to Others, to the Environment and Yourself.

These factors will each be explained in some detail in the book, but take a minute or so to speculate with me. Don't you, personally, desire to be in optimal physical and mental health, to be free of financial worries, to know that you have thinking skills you can use to deal with problems you will inevitably face, to behave responsibly toward others and the environment, and to take full responsibility for yourself and your actions?

If you have children or if you plan to have children, don't you want them to be physically and mentally healthy, to be financially secure, to be able to solve problems, to be responsible citizens and custodians of our environment, and to make the most out of the wonderful opportunity they have to be living here at this time in history? Wouldn't you want the same for all of your extended family? Wouldn't your neighbors be more fulfilled and happy if they were mastering the five factors? How about the people at your work, in your state, and in your country?

Let's get really crazy now: What if everyone in the world was physically and mentally healthy, was financially secure, was a good problem solver and critical thinker, treated others and the environment responsibly, and respected themselves as important and useful? Wouldn't that be a great place to live? Do you see why I say we need to be revolutionaries?

The diagram below is designed to show how integrated and related the five factors are.

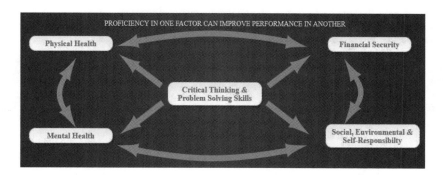

The Problem-Solving and Critical Thinking Skills factor seems to be the central factor of the five. The thinking skills will directly apply to the attainment and applications of the other four. However, if you don't have your physical health, you can be hampered in attaining other factors.

Of course, if your physical health is so bad that you are dead, the other factors don't matter much. Or you might have excellent physical health but your mental health is so poor that you can't reasonably function in other areas of your life. To me, financial security is one of the easiest to attain because you have so many variables that you can control, such as spending less or earning more. Being responsible would be the easiest to ignore because it mostly involves how you treat others and the environment. The long-term consequences to others and the environment are probably not as obvious as in the other factors. However, being responsible for yourself is a major key to your personal well-being, which is necessary if you are going to be able to be helpful to others. Take some time and play around with the factors. Look for different relationships. Which ones seem more important to you at this time in your life? Or do they all seem valuable enough to not warrant any prioritizations?

Here is a summary of some of the comments I have gotten when I have presented these five factors:

- It's so obvious, why haven't we been doing this all along?

- Why wasn't I taught this in school?

- Why didn't my parents teach me this?

- I wish I had known this forty years ago; my life would be a lot different today.

- I wish I had taught this to my kids; their lives would be a lot different today.

- I wish my boss would use these factors to run the business. They could also be used as a basis for his treatment of his employees.

- Wouldn't it be great if the big corporations used the five factors as a structure for running their businesses, dealing with employees, and how they treat their customers?

- What do you think would happen if those whom we have elected to represent us in government would use the five factors as guidelines for the legislation they propose and support?

- I wonder if we could incorporate these five factors into my religion or my church.

- Wouldn't it be great if national governments dealt with each other on the basis of the five factors?

- What other applications of the five factors can you think of?

The remainder of this book will consist of an explanation of the five factors and some key words and phrases you can use to do your own research in those areas you find most interesting, useful and applicable in your life. I suggest that you master the factors yourself first. Then you can be a model of their value and application. Also, as you master the factors, I hope you will refine and modify them. Make them better. At the very least, I hope you will take seriously and explore the question of "What's most important?"

I challenge you to have your own personal revolution and expand your successes to ever larger groups. As I write the challenge, I am reminded of my graduate philosophy class with the late Dr. Ernest Bayles, which seems to have relevance here. On the last day of a very enlightening semester class, he finished with a final summary and review of the various philosophies, their histories, and their implications. When he asked if there were any questions, I raised my hand and asked him where he thought philosophy would progress in the future.

His profound answer was, "That's up to you."

In the rest of this book I will introduce you to the five factors that I have isolated as an answer to the question "What's most important?" I am confident that if you strive to understand the concepts and skills and then apply them, to the best of your ability, to your life, then your life and the lives of those around you will be better for it. Will you try it?

That's up to you.

FACTOR 1

Gaining and Maintaining Physical Health

Our bodies are miracles, and we should treat them as such. Gaining and maintaining our physical health should be an obvious major priority for each of us. However, the vast majority of people unthinkingly take their bodies and health for granted … until something goes wrong. Then we ask our doctors to quickly and painlessly fix us. Most of us daily sabotage our personal miracles with unhealthy food and insufficient or inappropriate exercise. We don't know how our bodies work, and a lot of us don't care.

We, individually, must take primary responsibility for our bodies and our physical health. It is fascinating to learn how our bodies work, the power of prevention to minimize illness and injury, how our lifestyles are keys to our health, and how our physical health so profoundly influences all the other aspects of our lives. *We can't live forever, but we can intelligently adopt lifestyles that will help us live as long as possible and as healthy as possible.*

Before we get into some detailed information about how to adopt a positive physical health lifestyle, let's look as some behaviors that have negative impacts on human health. Take a look at the behaviors listed and honestly determine which, if any, you exhibit:

- Eating very fast.

- Eating large portions or never thinking about how much you eat.

- Eating off large plates and out of large bowls.

- Eating "family style" with all food on the table.

- Spending most of your day sitting down for long periods of time.

- Having hobbies and other avocations that do not involve exercise.

- Eating the same basic meals every day.

- Eating meals that mostly consist of meat and meat products such as sausage and cold cuts.

- Knowing you are overweight or obese but having no plan to lose weight.

- Going to the gym to look better, not to be healthier.

- Eating out several times a week.

- Buying concoctions that advertise they will make you really muscular even though you can't pronounce or identify the ingredients in them.

- Considering the word exercise to be a dirty word.

- Celebrating every holiday and family get-together with large quantities of holiday-type food and drink.

- Playing a sport such as golf, tennis, racquetball, or basketball once or twice a week for your exercise.

- Drinking several sugar-sweetened sodas a day.

- Eating mostly pre-prepared meals that come in cans or boxes when you eat at home.

- Never reading—or not knowing how to read—nutrition labels.

- Eating to get thinner, not to be healthier.

- Trying many diets to lose weight quickly but then gaining back the weight when you stop the diet.

- Researching your pet's diet more than your own.

- Eating what tastes good and ignoring nutritional value of the food.

- Watching a lot of television, playing lots of electronic games, and spending a lot of time surfing the Internet.

- Not making or taking time for exercise.

- Not making or taking the time to research information about nutrition or exercise.

- Eating white potatoes prepared as French fries as half your intake of all vegetables, like the average American does.

- Considering salads a side dish for rabbits.

How many of these undesirable health behaviors describe you or those close to you? Contrast these undesirable behaviors with the desirable behaviors detailed below. These ideas have been compiled over several decades of research, my personal testing, and my personal experience. Note that I am using the term "diet" to mean a long-term eating lifestyle, *not* a short-term crash diet to lose weight quickly.

NUTRITION

Primarily Eat a Variety of Natural, Plant-Based Foods in Moderation

We are bombarded with conflicting information about what we should eat. Corporate advertising, government food pyramids, diet peddlers, grandmas, doctors, and well-meaning friends all have ideas of what food is best for us. What should we feed ourselves and our children?

After spending decades of reading research studies, investigating crash diets and long-term lifestyles, watching people do unbelievably crazy things to lose weight, and seeing people throughout the world adopt the usual American diet only to get increasingly overweight and unhealthy, I decided that my personal nutrition lifestyle would be guided by three major concepts: **variety, natural plant-based food** and **moderation**. I have found this approach to be simple to remember and easy to implement. There is extensive research to support it, and I suggest you should try this approach yourself. *The best research is for you to try something and see if it works for you.* Here is how it works for me and a lot of other healthy people:

Natural Foods

Natural foods are those that have not been processed. Natural food is whole food. It is real food. It was not invented by a corporate scientist. If you grow a garden, you will have natural plant-based food. Natural food is what is in the produce section of your market. Most natural foods are plant-based. Natural food labels usually do not list ingredients that you don't recognize and can't pronounce. Natural foods can be found in the freezer section of your grocery store; these can be just as nutritious (unless they have added seasonings) as unfrozen fruits and vegetables—and they can be fresher and tastier.

Look for whole grains of all kinds, and shun the processed ones. For example, whole-wheat flour instead of white flour, and brown or black rice instead of white rice. Seeds and nuts are real plant-based foods. With a few exceptions—read the labels—foods that come in cans and boxes are processed and have added chemicals. You could eat most natural plant-based foods raw by hand in their natural state. Plant-based foods generally have much more nutrition per calorie than animal-based foods. Probably the best bang for your buck in real plant-based foods is green leafy vegetables, especially lettuces. They have the most nutrition for the fewest calories of anything you can eat.

What about animal-based foods? From the research I have seen, animals that are raised in huge corporate meat production-line plants are not natural because the animals are bred and fed to meet the corporations' requirement of attaining the largest profits possible. For instance, beef cattle are natural grass eaters. Their natural way of living and growing is to be in fields where they graze on grasses. Animals in big, commercial feed lots are in confined spaces, are fed large quantities of antibiotics and hormones, and are fed unnatural foods for them, such as grains to fatten them faster. The lack of normal grazing exercise and the abnormal diet changes their nutritional content and taste. The medications build up in the animals and are passed on to those who eat them. They are *not* natural. **Historically and internationally, as the consumption of animal-based products has increased, so has obesity and ill health. This is especially true in America.**

If you choose to add animal products in your variety of foods, look for those that have been raised like they were raised 150 years ago. Apply the same natural criteria to all animals, including poultry and fish, and all of their edible products like eggs, milk, and cheese. If you choose to eat animal-based foods, look for products from animals that have been raised as close to wild as possible. That will not be easy. Even if you are able to find naturally raised animal-based products, they will have less nutrition and more calories by weight than plant-based foods. Again, if you feel you must eat some animal products, eat a variety of them and eat them in very small quantities, because they are high in calories and relatively low in nutrition.

Variety

There is no one ideal diet, so variety is a necessary component of our diets. We don't know what future researchers will discover in foods that we don't know about today. What new vitamins, minerals, micronutrients, or other components will be found in foods in the future? There are probably many micronutrients that we simply haven't discovered yet. We can protect ourselves by eating a very wide variety of natural, plant-based foods to increase the probability that we are getting all the nutrients we know about and also those we don't know about. Another plus is that variety in our diets gives us many textures, tastes, and colors in our meals.

Many people, especially guys, describe themselves as meat-and-potatoes kind of people. Give them a huge steak with some mashed potatoes and gravy, and they are happy. That's the way they were taught to eat, and that is the way they intend to always eat. Some different meats, and different ways of fixing the white potatoes, are about as much variety as they will tolerate. This kind of repetitious lifestyle of eating is hazardous to their health because a healthy diet consists of more than just the nutrients in meats and potatoes. In fact, these kinds of meals are woefully lacking in nutrition and greatly abundant in calories. *Eating a restricted and repetitious diet, especially if it is centered around animal-based products, is the same as going to the gym to get in better physical condition and only doing biceps curls.*

Moderation

Modern world problems with obesity and health problems have many causes, but one of the most important and easy to determine is the one of quantity of eating. For example, on a vacation trip in Costa Rica I took a few years ago, all meals were provided. They were tasty, large meals; or they were huge buffets where we could choose anything we wanted in any quantity we wanted. Many people ate large portions. We were on a bus and getting very little exercise for those ten days. Even though the meals were very good and very big, many people additionally purchased high-calorie snacks and drinks to consume as we rode around on the bus. *They were eating almost all of the time.* And they looked it. This is an obvious example of how we can easily develop habits of enormous food consumption and not even be aware of the damage we are doing to our bodies and our health.

Restaurants, especially those known for fast food, have tended to increase portion sizes. It's a better bargain to get the jumbo, super, triple-decker, whopper, gigantic, titanic burger than to get the regular one, right? We are always looking for bargains.

What are your eating habits? Here are some ways I have learned to deal with portion size based on research and my own trial and error:

- I seldom eat out because I like to prepare my own food, know what is in my food, and control my portions. I cook at home because I know the cleanliness of my kitchen and utensils. If I do eat out, I usually split a meal with a companion or eat only about half and take the rest home.

- When I prepare a meal for myself to be eaten at one time, I use a small skillet, bowl or microwave dish for preparing the food to deliberately control the portion size. When I make a smoothie, I usually fill the blender no more than two-thirds full. I always accompany any meal with water. I try to eat slowly to fill up while I am still eating. For example, this morning I had a whole-grain multigrain toast slice with cashew butter, avocado, and banana slices on it. However, I ate it with a knife and fork, cutting off each bite. I used to gobble down toast held in my hand in a few seconds and was still hungry when I finished.

- I very seldom eat what are thought of as usual desserts such as pie, cake, and ice cream. Dessert, if eaten, is in very small cups just to sample it. I will eat whole fruit for a refreshing dessert. I just don't eat desserts that contain any addition of sugars. After years of not eating sugary foods, I have no cravings for them.

- Many people find that using smaller plates and smaller eating utensils cuts down on the food they eat. Also, some people use taller, thinner glasses because they give the illusion of containing more liquid.

- Many families have traditions of gathering at holidays, birthdays, and other celebratory occasions. These usually involve lots of food and drink that are festive but not necessarily nutritious, especially for the calories consumed. These gatherings can be food orgies. We don't have to eat and drink too much, but this is just what we do at family and holiday gatherings.

- The same is true of office parties, company parties, and other social gatherings, especially if they are pot-luck-, family-, or buffet-style where you can go back for more as often as you want.

- My observation: There is a high correlation between overeating and watching television. Enough said.

- The same can be said for any spectator events such as professional sports, movies, college sports, and any other event where we sit for hours watching someone else perform. They are performing, and we are sitting and watching and probably eating and drinking high-calorie food, not nutritious food. Sound familiar?

- Do you nibble and taste the food as you are cooking?

- Do you eat food left on the family table as you clear the dishes for washing?

Eating in moderation is just a set of habits that we can learn and practice. The ideas above are just a start. I am sure that with a little creative thought and research, you can come up with others. *Eating in moderation should be part of our lifestyles; not something we do over a few days to quickly lose a few pounds.*

Preparation Ideas

When my wife died, a lot of things changed in my life. One of the minor changes was that I was now totally in charge of my diet, grocery shopping, menu-planning, and meal preparation. I had usually done most of the grocery shopping, but my wife had done almost all the cooking. I could boil the water, chop up salads, and make the garlic toast to go with her lasagna. But now I was totally on my own in the kitchen. What to do?

I started watching television shows where chefs of all kinds demonstrate how to cook. I started reading cookbooks. I was especially amazed (and still am) at how the chefs could coordinate the various parts of a meal and bring them, at the right temperature, to the table at the same time. I was equally jealous of how they knew what different blends of spices, flavors, and textures would taste like as a finished product.

This orchestration of meats, vegetables, grains, fruits, nuts, seeds, spices, and liquids was obviously the result of years of study, practice, trial and error, adjustments, and professional knowledge. Wait! I'm already in my seventies and don't want to take the time at this point to learn all these culinary tricks. So I started to solve the problem of how to prepare a variety of natural foods in *simple* and *easy* ways that can be adjusted to a variety of tastes. Without going into all the discovery details, I came upon my solution: the one-dish meal.

As I thought about it, one-dish meals have always been my favorite way to eat. Stews, thick soups, big salads, stir-fries, smoothies, pizzas, tostadas, and everything else that can be put on one plate or in one bowl or glass and consumed as a full meal have many advantages. One-dish meals are perfect for today's busy schedules.

Preparation could consist of putting together a variety of natural foods, seasoning them, maybe cooking them, and serving them in reasonable proportions. For example, you can make a stew with just about any combination of a variety of vegetables, beans, grains, and other natural ingredients you desire or have on hand. Add some seasoning and liquid of your choice and you have a meal. When it is finished to taste, you serve in sizes appropriate to those being served. Individuals can then add more seasonings to their portions if they so desire. Your cooking cleanup is one pot and some utensils. Pretty simple and easy compared with the stress of serving a meal that requires you to coordinate several separate dishes to all arrive at the table at the same time at the peak of their flavor and presentation. Let's have some mercy for the cooks and help them reduce their kitchen stress by preparing one-dish meals … especially if we are the cooks.

The one-dish meal is ideal nutritionally because you have thousands of combinations (a variety) of natural ingredients to choose from every time you put one together. You can be creative and surely find some combinations that will satisfy even the pickiest of eaters. You can have a few ingredients or you can have many. For example, you might use different combinations of frozen vegetables and beans, some low-sodium cooking broth, tomato sauce, a can or two of diced tomatoes, maybe a favorite whole grain, and perhaps a small amount of meat in a pot with your favorite seasonings. Let it cook until the ingredients are cooked to your satisfaction and serve. You can feel comfortable that you have provided a nutritious meal that can promote good health rather than hinder it.

Some Additional Ideas about Nutrition

- **Things I would not feed myself or anyone else:** sausage, wieners, almost all "prepared meals" made by corporations that come in cans or are frozen, anything made with white flour or loaded with fat or sugar, and anything that has ingredients I can't pronounce. Look at the labels!

- **Why do parents feed their kids junk food?** If you shouldn't eat it, neither should your kids. We are increasingly finding eating-related diseases in younger and younger kids. Nobody should junk food it even if it tastes good or is cheap, no matter how quiet it keeps the kids.

- **Carbohydrates and protein** have four calories per gram, alcohol has seven calories, and fats have nine calories. Most plant-based foods fall into the lowest category of calories per gram. Animal products are higher-calorie foods. In addition to being lower in calories, the plant-based foods have far more nutrients. Strive to eat the most nutritious foods that have the fewest calories.

- **Usually, the more colorful the plant-based food is the more nutritious it is.**

- **Concentrations of sugars, fats, and salt** are the main hooks the corporate food industry uses to lure us to purchase the non-natural concoctions they market as food.

- **Crock-Pots are safe and easy to use**, and they enable you to cook when you aren't at home.

- **Healthy eating is important** to physical health, but body movement (exercise) should be considered equally so.

- **It is better to eat the whole fruit or vegetable** rather than to juice it, because fiber and some nutrients are lost in juicing.

- **When you make changes in your diet** such as shifting to a plant-based emphasis, you might experience some stomach upset and gas. It is natural and will go away as your body adjusts. So phase in your change slowly but surely.

- **Make water your favorite drink**. It is cheap, safe, and necessary for your health. You are mostly made of it. Be wary of water with corporate-added "stuff." It is more expensive and designed to get you hooked on the added ingredients—which are added to improve the corporate profit margin, not to improve your health.

- **Beware of all the sugary sodas,** artificially sweetened sodas, "energy" drinks, "power" drinks, and other manufactured brews advertised to get you to buy them. Read the labels. They are full of sugars, caffeine, and other chemicals to make you temporarily feel stimulated. They are designed to sell, not to make you healthier. Be an informed consumer. I don't touch them.

- **If you choose to eat some animal-based products**, make the serving size as small as you can. A common suggestion for meats is a serving size no larger than a deck of cards; for cheeses, a serving size no larger than a 1-inch cube.

- **Frozen foods**—those that are only the natural food without added corporate ingredients—have been picked at their freshest and then quickly flash frozen so their nutrition and flavors are preserved. You don't have to worry about them going bad like you do fresh produce. Just use what you need, reseal the package, and put the remainder back in the freezer. As a single person, I find this both very convenient and less expensive.

- **Recent studies indicate that vegetables** are only about 10 percent of the average American's diet. Half of that 10 percent is white potatoes, mostly in the form of French fries and mashed potatoes. White potatoes are among the least nutritious of the vegetables.

- **A big part of making one-dish meals is the seasonings you use.** I am slowly learning some of the combinations of spices that I like the most. I have read cookbooks, watched chefs on television, and talked with restaurant workers when I like the taste of a meal and want to replicate it. Although this has been useful, it is just as useful and also fun to explore the already-blended spices in the international section of your local grocery stores. Many of these spice blends are salt-free. Buy samples of the blends and try them. Maybe you can revise a blend and make it better. Many of us have found that Thai, Indian, Chinese, Mexican, and cuisines from other regions of the world use spices that are different, delicious, and give additional varieties of tastes to our dishes.

- **Be aware of your triggers that make you want to eat even if you are not hungry.** Some common triggers are television, stress, procrastination, worry, boredom, and reading. These can become unhealthy habits when activities or emotions get paired with eating. That association of two things—for example, television and eating—can become a habit that has very unhealthy results.

- **The research I have read has led me to eat the leanest of meats** on the few occasions that I do eat meat. Likewise, I seldom eat dairy products; but when I do, they are low fat or nonfat, and I use just a small amount for the flavor. Treat animal-based foods as condiments: just a bit for the flavor you like.

- **We need some fats in a complete diet.** Cooking oils such as olive, canola, and coconut are pure fat (120 calories per tablespoon), so minimize their use. Avocados, nuts, and seeds are seen as more nutritious sources of the *good* fats, and they contain many other nutrients as well.

- **Be very wary of diets that concentrate on a small group of foods.** Be skeptical of magical claims for one food or group of foods. Be wary of any of *the secrets of* *nutrition* gimmicks being peddled. Beware of supplements that are sold as having super curative powers or as able to prevent you from getting some disease. Beware of infomercials and advertisements that tell you to ask your doctor to prescribe a certain drug for you. These are ploys to sell you products, not to make you healthier.

- **Don't take nutritional advice** (or any other advice) from someone who obviously isn't following it.

What I am suggesting as a nutritional lifestyle is meant to lead to better overall health. It is *not* to build huge masses of muscle or to make you a professional athlete. It is meant as a starting point for people who want to explore reasonable, simple and easy changes in how they feed their bodies and the bodies of those who eat the food they prepare. It is meant to be revised, adapted, modified, experimented with by you, and made better in as many ways as possible.

Let me end with a story to illustrate a couple of points. When I was a little kid, my parents and I lived on a small farm outside Kansas City where we grew and raised almost all we ate. It was natural food and mostly plant-based. We bought very little food from corporate America, mainly because we couldn't afford it. Mom, Dad, and I were healthy by any standards. One day I was playing with a neighbor, Jerry Ruby. At noon, his mom brought us a little lunch while we sat on the swing. I'll never forget it. The lunch consisted of a hot dog on a white bun that had mustard and catsup on it, a sack of potato chips, a large helping of pork and beans, and a bottle of pop. I had never eaten those foods in that combination before. I was in taste-bud heaven! *As I finished the meal I declared that when I was rich enough, this would be the only food I would eat for the rest of my life.* I was sure that nothing could possibly be this good-tasting!

Point one, that meal was a non-deliberate combination of the three corporate hooks currently used to entice you and me to buy manufactured foods. *This meal was full of fat, salt, and sugars, all delivered at the same time. That meal was as instantly addictive to me then as crack cocaine is to a first-time user.* I needed more of that stuff and couldn't wait to get home to tell my parents what to put on the grocery list.

Point two, my parents would not listen to my pleas for us to eat meals like Mrs. Ruby fixed for me. They had some lame excuse like it was too expensive. I had to continue to eat those natural foods until I left home many years later. By that time I had forgotten about Mrs. Ruby's meal of ecstasy. Thankfully.

EXERCISE

Your Body—Use It or Lose It—A Case for Variety and Moderation in Physical Exercise

Our bodies have 650 or so muscles. The generations before us used their bodies far more than most of us do today. They walked more. They worked on farms, in manufacturing plants, and at other jobs that did not use the technology of today. In fact, the purpose of many inventions throughout history has been to take the physical activity out of all types of work. We in the industrially developed parts of the world have been very successful in reducing the amount of physical exercise that we must do. However, we now have study after study that tell us most Americans do not get nearly enough exercise. Our work, hobbies, and other discretionary time normally do not involve physical exercise. An old friend, Bennie, a professional clarinet player, once said, "What makes it for you breaks it for you." Although I think his saying should be modified to "What makes it for you *sometimes* breaks it for you," it fits this case. People are increasingly less healthy as we increasingly reduce the actual physical work we do. Ironically, we are now inventing machines and activities to help us exercise more. We have gone from the need to work less to the need to work (work out) more. I think we can find a happy medium.

I presume that you are reading this because you are interested in being physically healthy. *The suggestions below are designed for those who exercise to be healthy.* They are not for those who want to be bodybuilders with abnormally large muscles or weight lifters who push their bodies to and sometimes beyond their limits. The suggestions below are based on my research, observations, and personal experience. Here are some suggestions for healthy exercise:

- **The focus of your exercise should be variety and moderation.** You want to periodically and consistently exercise as many of your muscles as you can, but you want to do it in moderation. You do not need to strain every muscle until it fails. You want to use the muscles, not abuse them. Strain muscles moderately or maybe a little more than moderately. You don't need to hurt. Strive for a level of strength that allows you to do what you need to do physically and then just a little bit more ... just in case.

- **If you do not exercise, then your body will atrophy.** Your bones will lose strength. Your muscles will lose strength. Your heart will lose strength. Less blood will flow to your brain, and you will lose some mental agility. When you lose muscle strength in the core of your body, you will lose some of your ability to balance yourself. If you don't exercise for a long period of time, tasks will become harder to do, and some tasks you used to do will become impossible. You can't lift it, climb it, or carry it. It is too much for you. You are not strong enough, don't have enough breath, lose your grip, feel sluggish most of the time, and don't like what you see in the mirror. And you have a nagging feeling of guilt that follows you wherever you go.

- **Over a long period of inactivity and poor diet, you'll be more likely to have the life-threatening combination of withering body and increasing weight.** Without exercise your bones get weaker, muscles get weaker, and the heart gets weaker—and they all must support an ever-increasing body mass. You are like an old car that is not maintained. The tires are nearly flat, the oil is low, the springs and shocks are shot, it has inferior gas, it has never been lubricated but it must keep hauling more people, plus heavier luggage and a pile of boxes of heavy materials on the roof. Eventually, that car is going to break down, possibly in a drastic way and or even fatally. The same is true for you if you eat nonnutritious foods and don't maintain your body by following a reasonable program of exercise.

- **I love to watch little kids in the park.** They will spontaneously burst into a run. They instinctively run, jump, climb, slide, and create all kinds of other things to do that involve moving their bodies. During all this movement, they always seem to be smiling and laughing. What happens to them as they get older? They go to school, where they sit most of the time. Many schools now have no recesses or organized programs involving physical activity for all the kids.

- However, most schools have sports programs where a few people play and most watch. Kids go home and do homework, watch television, play highly addicting video games, text, talk on the phone, and often snack on junk foods. When families do things together it is often watching movies, sporting events or television, or having family get-togethers where copious amounts of food (usually not healthy) and beverages (usually empty calories) are consumed. Recreation is often motorized, using ATVs, motorboats, Jet Skis, motorcycles, snowmobiles, and other forms of self-propelled recreational "toys." Schools, families, and our society in general do not foster physical activity. *If you are going to be more like the kids in the park, you will have to be different from the vast majority of Americans today.*

- People often tell me that they are too old to start exercising. Many scientific studies show that people in their 90s have gained measurable health benefits by starting and following a program of exercise at that late age. **Chronological age is no excuse for not exercising.**

- Walking—and variations including running, hiking, climbing, and anything where you move your body in its upright position—puts stress on your bones and makes them stronger. The same is true of any resistance exercise that puts pressure on your bones. **Muscles, bones, and brains all need to be used in a variety of ways.**

- **Guys, don't overdo it. The biggest muscles don't mean the best health.** I am sure there is a point of diminishing returns in muscle building. I have observed men who can hardly walk because their legs are so overly muscled. I have seen men who don't seem to be able to put their arms down to their sides because their shoulders and upper arms were so oversized. I have seen other overmuscled men who were unable to properly play a sport because their huge muscles didn't allow them to move with freedom and flexibility.

- I am also suspicious of all the potions you guys take before, during, and after your workouts. Do you know what is in that stuff? Finally, my informal poll of the ladies I think you might be trying to impress indicates that huge muscles are not girl magnets. I know you guys probably won't stop your bodybuilding because, being guys, you think bigger is always better. We guys also think that if a few drops of cologne is good, then a quarter-cup has got to be better. Neither is true, and neither will impress the vast majority of those you want to impress.

- **If you go to a gym or other public place** to work out, wash your hands when you enter so you don't bring any germs in, and wash your hands when you leave so you don't take any out. Remember that all of that equipment is touched by a lot of people, and there are a lot of them who are less than sanitary in their habits.

- **Listen to your body.** Your body talks to you all the time. *If you have a pain, it is your body telling you that something is wrong.* Whether the pain is a headache, sting, throb, ache, pounding sensation, stabbing pain, dull pain or "worst pain you ever experienced," it is your body trying to tell you something. It is usually signaling that you need to stop what you are doing and find out what is wrong. That pain might be a signal that you have strained, pulled, torn or separated a muscle, or that you've done some other damage to your body. You should stop and find out what it is. *You should not "bravely" (stupidly) work through it or "play through the pain" and possibly make the strain into a tear. Your* *body will tell you it is not macho to be stupid.* I know: I personally heard mine tell me that. I haven't found females trying to be "macho" in this way, but it applies to us all. Equally bad is the person who has an exercise-related pain but takes a painkiller to mask the pain and doesn't try to find the cause. If you won't or can't get medical help to find the cause of an injury, then treat yourself using the RICE method. RICE is an acronym that stands for Rest, Ice, Compression, and Elevation.

I mentioned headaches above. I do not get headaches since I follow the nutrition and exercise programs I am advocating. I have not had a headache for forty or more years, and that last one was self-induced and liquid-related.

• **Get in the habit of using every opportunity possible to exercise your body.** Of course you can join a gym and have a trainer design an exercise plan for you. You can read books and magazines on the subject, join clubs, watch videos, and do all sorts of other things to develop more formal, structured types of exercise programs. But what about all the other informal, everyday opportunities for exercise that add up over time? Here are some ideas that I have done and seen work:

  • Walk whenever you can, such as to the mailbox, to a nearby store, or in the airport.

  • Use the stairs instead of the elevator or escalator. I try to get hotel rooms on floors four to seven so I can use the stairs for moderate exercise.

  • Play family games that involve exercise. Go hiking as a family.

  • At the office, walk down the hall and talk directly to a colleague instead of emailing, texting, or phoning.

  • Take a short walk for a break from your desk work at least every hour or so.

- **Think like your muscles to gauge how much you want to strain yourself.** If I am a muscle and I never have to move more than to press the button on the remote, text on my smartphone, or lift a fork, I have no reason to get stronger. However, if someone is straining me by making me lift weight heavier than I am used to, I will try to get bigger and stronger in anticipation of the heavier future weight. *So the formula is no strain or less strain on the muscles equals smaller, weaker muscles. Conversely, more strain on the muscles equals larger, stronger muscles.* It is up to you to decide how strong you need to be or want to be. My preference is in the medium range that Goldilocks would call "just right."

- **The physically healthy person usually has a more-or-less moderate build and some moderate muscle definition as a result of moderate exercise of as many muscles as possible.** This, of course, is accompanied by a nutrition lifestyle that emphasizes maximum nutrition for the fewest calories. That was discussed earlier. Note that the human body has an upright position. Bones are stacked on bones with pads between them. This signals to me that humans who weigh less put less strain on their upright skeletons, and that the heavier we are the more wear and tear we put on our skeletons. The same is true of most of our organs: They thrive better if they do not have to constantly compensate for the added strain of extra weight or obesity.

- **There are many ways to get healthy exercise. I have personally found that going to a gym or health club is best for me.** I can use machines that are designed for specific muscle groups so I can plan workouts that use the maximum number of muscles in each set of repetitions. I can adjust machines to the amount of resistance I desire. In larger clubs they have many types of machines for resistance training, aerobic and yoga classes, bikes, swimming pools, basketball courts, racquetball courts, and organized leagues. The cost of these gyms or health clubs is well worth it when you consider that our physical health has to be one of the most, if not the most, important assets we have. Your health should be a personal priority.

- **There are usually trainers in these health clubs who hopefully can assist you, although there is tremendous variance in the quality of their knowledge.** Do some health and exercise research online or at the library, subscribe to a magazine that deals with health knowledge, or maybe start a group of people who want to do research on their health and then share it among yourselves. You can also hire a good trainer and learn the proper techniques for meeting your goals. Then after you have mastered them you can do them on your own.

- **I have found that it is much more difficult to do exercise at home.** There are always distractions. There is little or no equipment to work with, no one to ask for advice, and always something that has be done. I can't tell you how many times I have seen people buy a piece of exercise equipment to use at home and discard it in a few weeks or months. Even for those who consistently use the machine, it will not provide the variety of exercises they need.

  If you have to do your exercising at home, I would suggest a set of dumbbells that go from five pounds or so up to maybe thirty-five to fifty. Then set up a program where you use these for a full body workout. You will probably also need a bench that can incline. You can get your cardio workout outside by walking, hiking, climbing, or jogging. If you are unable to leave your home to get your cardio exercise, then you might look into a rowing machine, elliptical trainer, or treadmill. There are plenty of used ones for sale.

- Your exercise schedule should include both resistance and cardio training in generally equal amounts about every other day. I find 1 to 1½ hours per workout is good for me. You will have to choose what is right for you depending on your schedule, the demands of job and family, and your goals. It is a good idea to tell your doctor what you are planning to do, especially if you have pre-existing physical problems or have not exercised for some time. Be aware that many doctors are not knowledgeable about the specifics of exercising, so you need to be responsible for developing an exercise plan. You then start any new program slowly and with caution.

- **Vary the intensity of your exercises.** For example, if you are lifting a weight of fifteen pounds for a certain exercise for two sets of fifteen repetitions, then every third or fourth time you do the exercise you might want to do two sets of ten repetitions at twenty pounds. You can experiment with the schedule specifics, but varying the weights keeps the muscles guessing. The same would be true for your cardiovascular workouts. Don't go at the same speed all the time. Go faster sometimes, but shorter distances. Go slower sometimes, but for longer distances. Go up and down hills for more intensity than when you exercise on level ground. If you use cardio machines in a gym, change elevations, intensities and times. When people speak of interval training, they are describing the technique of cardio exercise that consists of a shorter interval of very fast (anaerobic) exercise followed by a longer interval of less strenuous exercise (aerobic) exercise like walking or jogging. For example, if you are riding one of the bicycles at your gym, you might pedal at 70 rpm for two minutes and then at 100 rpm for one minute. You need to experiment with what works best for you.

- **Riding a street bike is not much exercise if you ride on a flat surface, and it can be very dangerous, especially on roads or streets.** Riding hills or mountain trails is different; it can be very demanding exercise. However, you can exercise on hills and trails probably more safely by hiking or jogging.

- **You get in shape to play sports; you don't play sports to get in shape**. People whose only exercise is to play a sport once or twice a week get very little benefit from it and are more likely to hurt themselves. This is true of almost all sports. Sports can be very intense and have bursts of intensity that put great strain on a few muscles and joints. These brief bursts of intensity require that the body be carefully trained to withstand those stresses. The weekend warrior who is normally sedentary throughout the week and then plays his or her sport on the weekend will inevitably have something strained, torn, or detached sooner or later. The repetition or the intensity of the sport will be too much for the body that has been sitting behind a desk the rest of the week. Watch the people who get their exercise only through infrequent sports. They do not get stronger, healthier, or "more buff." But they will frequently have sprains, strains, tears, and various surgeries. Nike is wrong. *Don't "Just Do It." Do It Intelligently!*

- **If you are going to play sports, play a variety of them.** I think I personally am healthier because I played a variety of sports and worked out in a variety of ways throughout my long life. As I moved from one sport to another, I never did one long enough to have it harm me. I played football, baseball, and basketball in high school. Luckily, although I certainly didn't think so when it happened, I was badly injured in the homecoming game of my senior year and was not a candidate for a college team. When I realized I was not going to be able to play college ball, I decided that academics would have to be my strength when I moved on to the university. After that I got my physical exercise by working out and playing tennis and racquetball, running, walking, and hiking. I now daily walk to the gym and do controlled resistance training and cardio exercises. *I have been lucky I had that variety. I admit I didn't plan it that way but now recognize it is a good plan. I pass it on to you.* At age seventy-eight as of this writing, I am physically functioning as I did at fifty or younger.

If you have children and they want to play sports, have them play a variety of sports. Concentrating on one sport from a young age means the stresses and repetitive motions of that one sport are constant potential problems for your child's health. There is a reason why professional athletes have short careers and often live their lives with pains, and physical and mental problems, after they retire. A lifetime of that one sport can just be too much for the human body to take, even for a professional athlete with the latest in training methods and technologies. Isn't that similar to what we do with our youngsters who are not fully developed physically and mentally, who are coached by volunteers with a huge variation of competencies, and who often have inferior equipment but have essentially the same kinds of traumas as the professional players of the same sports?

- **Don't be taken in by the powders, potions, bars, supplements, and other concoctions that are supposed to melt off your fat, increase your stamina, add muscle mass, make your workout easier, or take years off your age. These products are from corporations producing products to make a profit.** These concoctions are seldom tested scientifically. There is little or no guarantee of their safety. There is no guarantee that they will do what they say they will do. They are often high-calorie products that add more calories to your diet than you burn up in your workout. *If you want to be safe and get the most health out of your workout, drink plain water.* Don't fall for all the advertising and hype by the corporations. Read the labels. Do some research. Use common sense.

Again I encourage you to do research on your own. What I have written should be a good start and give you some ideas of what you want to know more about. Here are some key terms and phrases you can use to do some deeper digging into how to gain and maintain your physical health:

- Live as long as possible, as healthy as possible.

- Take responsibility for your health.

- Diets.

- Lifestyles.

- Physical activity.

- Balance.

- Variety.

- Moderation.

- Research and media reporting on health issues.

- Think like your body.

- Medications.

- Basic anatomy.

- Basic physiology.

- Empty calories.

- Nutrition.

- Unknown nutrients.

- Portion size problems.

- Obsessions with food and exercise.

- Spectator or participant.

- Sports (youth, lifelong).

- Sedentary lifestyle.

- Standard American diet (SAD).

- Sex, fun, and STDs.

- Lifestyle analysis.

- Junk food.

- Fats, sugars, and salt are out to get you.

- Are you eating to live or living to eat?

- Advertising.

- Food pyramids.

- Expectations.

- Failure.

- Enjoyment.

- Habits.

- Simple and complex carbohydrates.

- Processed versus "real" foods.

- Motivation.

- The power of moving our bodies.

- Teach and model good lifestyles early.

- You are a role model for health, good or bad.

- You *do* have the time.

- What are your priorities?

- Listen to your body.

- Ouch, I need a pill!

- Self–medicating.

- Corporations are very worried about your health.

- Feel safe.

- Sometimes you have to be "selfish."

- A different kind of child abuse.

- If it isn't in the house, I can't eat it.

FACTOR 2

Gaining and Maintaining Mental Health

He was a high school senior. He was an elected class officer; had started on the football, baseball, and basketball teams; was dating a beautiful, smart, popular girl; was an honor roll student; had a full scholarship to college; and, in general, had a life that most people in the world would envy. Yet that young man who had everything going for him was unhappy much of the time. Why? He unwittingly dwelled on the minuscule part of his life that was not to his liking. He missed enjoying the vast majority of his life, which was nearly perfect by any standard.

That high school senior was me. I could play a great football game against our school's archrival, but when the game was over, I would dwell on the few instances where I should have waited a second longer to let the receiver get free before I threw a pass that couldn't be caught. Or I would dwell on the time I missed a tackle that I should have made.

To be clear, I wasn't a sullen, unhappy person all the time. However, my own negative thinking caused me to lose out on much of the enjoyment of those formative years, and it bred a mindset and habit of emphasizing the negatives in my life. It took a lot of study and mindset changes before I was able to replace that destructive habit.

I don't want that to happen to you.

You can be in great physical health, be financially secure, and be a responsible citizen yet not enjoy life because of the way you think about yourself and the events that happen to you. It's been estimated that more than ninety percent of who we are is what we think. Yet formal education seldom, if ever, teaches even the basics of mental health. The purpose of this chapter is to give you some fundamentals for gaining and maintaining mental health and to encourage you to use some of your discretionary time to explore other topics relating to how we think and how that thinking results in our behaviors.

First, a word of explanation:

In terms of the Five Factors as covered in this book, mental health does not refer to clinically diagnosed mental illnesses. Rather, mental health means realistically thinking in ways that lead us to happier, more satisfying, productive and socially responsible lives.

As this chapter began, I showed how my emphasis on the few negatives in my early life was detrimental to enjoying the many positives I should have been celebrating. Now let's look at this from a different angle. How can your thinking influence the way you deal with major setbacks in life?

The late actor Christopher Reeve, who played Superman in the 1978 movie of that name, unfortunately faced this very problem. Rendered quadriplegic by a tragic riding accident, he spent the remainder of his life in a wheelchair. Yet despite the devastating nature of his injuries, he had suffered no permanent cognitive damage. His mind was soon as clear as ever, but he couldn't walk, tie his shoelaces, or feed himself. Even talking was difficult until he learned how to pace himself between machine-assisted breaths.

Although his first post-accident thoughts centered on the desire to die, Reeves soon changed his mind and went on to lead a challenging yet meaningful new life. He inspired other quadriplegics, participated in breakthrough research, played the role of a paralyzed man in a movie, and even fathered another child. He realized that his shriveled body didn't define him. Extremely intelligent, and with a self-effacing sense of mischievous humor, he was still a husband, a father, an actor, and a man. Significantly, he wrote about his post-accident life in a book titled *I'm Still Me.*

Reeve's courage in the face of overwhelming adversity was based on his decision to emphasize the positives in his life: the mental faculties he was still able to use and the things he was still able to do. Many, if not most, people in his situation would have given up and lived lives of regret and depression, but he chose to emphasize the tools with which he survived. Rather than dwell on the past, he chose to deal realistically with the present and even looked forward to his future. In a nationally televised interview, he told millions of viewers that with the help of new technology and medical research, he expected to walk again. When Barbara Walters asked, "What if you don't?" he smiled and said, "Then I won't."

That last statement is what I call *realistic optimism.* While remaining determinedly optimistic about his future, he was also realistic enough to be prepared for an undesirable outcome.

In another example, a woman I know came home from work and found that her house had been burglarized. While waiting for the police, she did not allow herself to become a weeping victim but instead deliberately focused on the positive aspects of the situation. Although her jewelry and laptop computer were gone, nothing had been broken or damaged other than the entry window. Most importantly, neither she nor her pets had been injured, and she had wisely taken out insurance for replacement value of her belongings. By emphasizing the positive side of the burglary event rather than dwelling on its negative aspects, she was able to concentrate on what she needed to do to move forward. When the check finally came from the insurance company, she used it to buy a better, newer laptop and get the sporty new car she had always wanted.

"That car adds more to my life than the jewelry ever did," she says now. "Whenever I find myself thinking of the burglary, or of anything that was taken, I just remind myself of that nice new car in the garage that I wouldn't otherwise have." And she jokes about the stolen computer, which had gone back to the factory three times for repairs before it was stolen. "The burglar got a lemon and I got a new Apple," she said.

What You Think About Tends to Come About

Probably the best example of this principle is my friend, Jason, who suffered brain damage leading to cerebral palsy when he was accidentally dropped as a premature infant.

"When I was a kid growing up, my disability was a lot more noticeable than it is now," he said. "Other kids made fun of me, and the bullies gave me a hard time. It was pretty rough." Being bullied and ridiculed by his peers triggered anger and a desire to get even. Many people with a limitation as severe as Jason's simply give up. They only see and think about their limitations. Many spend the rest of their lives on disability payments, watching television and feeling sorry for themselves. Not Jason.

"Rather than believe doctors and other people who stressed my limitations and talked about all the things I couldn't or shouldn't do, I just went out and did those things," he said. "It was a mindset I got into, and it got stronger and stronger. I took up boxing and karate and basketball, and I also did a lot of physical training. I even learned to drive a stick shift."

Jason's thinking was focused on what he could do now and what he planned to do in the future. As he continued to think about getting stronger and more agile, he found and participated in more activities. When his body turned leaner and more muscular from all the concentrated exercise and sports activity, students who had originally bullied him or laughed at him turned into admirers and even friends.

As this book is being written, Jason is a young married father with a beautiful wife and three children. He is training and seeking sponsors to enable him to compete in the long jump and other events at the 2016 Paralympics in Rio de Janeiro. He hopes that by competing in those games, he can gain recognition and funding for an organization he is starting to assist others who have cerebral palsy. He also wants to demonstrate by his own example that if people with disabilities can focus their thoughts on a positive future and mentally see themselves being what they want to be, that positive future will be more likely to happen. "My competing and doing well in the Paralympics would inspire disabled kids to see that kind of achievement as a possibility for themselves," he said. "They would then have the confidence to see other possibilities in their own lives."

"I want to show people you can do anything you put your mind to," he said. "Everyone has certain disabilities, whether financial, physical, or otherwise, and I want to inspire people to overcome those limitations, whatever they are. And I specifically want to launch camps and clinics for children who have cerebral palsy. The thrill of seeing them achieve their dreams will be my greatest reward!"

Jason has replaced self-defeating thoughts of being a victim and accepting limitations with his favorite phrase, "There's always a way."

Mental Health and Stress

At this point I am going to do two things at once. I will introduce you to several key components of mental health, but I will do that as I apply them to what we have come to call "stress." Since stress plays such a large negative role in daily modern life, I think it will be doubly useful if I show how we can prevent, reduce, control, and even use stress by utilizing key mental health principles. First, let me explain just what stress is and how it affects us.

Some Stress Basics:
It's natural to have stress.

When we encounter a situation we perceive as both undesirable and out of our control, we say it is stressful. To gain some control over the situation, our bodies automatically make rapid adjustments that allow us to deal with the situation physically, much like our ancient ancestors did. That is, we get a series of physical "boosts" to better help us either avoid the situation (run away from it as fast as we can) or meet it head on (physically attack the threat or defend ourselves), as described in the familiar phrase "fight or flight."

For example, the caveman who met a giant bear on the narrow path had little choice other than to either run away from the bear or fight it. There was no room for negotiation. The only negotiation was the most-rapid-as-possible negotiation of the path back to the safety of the cave. If retreat wasn't an available alternative, he would have to fight the bear, humans don't often win.

To provide optimal survival possibilities to the caveman, his body sped up his metabolic rate, heart rate, and breathing rate; it tensed his muscles, caused arteries to spasm, and increased platelet-clumping ability. These were adaptations that gave the caveman quick energy, provided him with a denser shield of muscle, and decreased the chances of profuse bleeding. Our ancestors, who survived many crises of this kind, evolved physiological systems that performed these changes especially well. Those who had bodies unable to make these quick adaptations didn't survive. We have thus inherited physiological systems that are quite efficient at making adjustments during crisis situations. Lucky us!

Times have changed, sort of, however. Our caveman ancestors spent most of their days concerned with the most basic elements of living. Most of their lives were spent in the routines of looking for food and resting. But once in a while they encountered dangers that required the run-or-fight mechanism to be activated. If they survived the crisis, the danger would pass and their bodies would return to normal. That is, the metabolic breathing and heart rates would slow down, the muscles and arteries would relax, and platelets would not clump as easily. In other words, the caveman had stress, but it was not very frequent and it was over rather quickly, and afterward the caveman went back to a relatively stress-free life.

Today, the run-or-fight defense mechanism is still part of human physiology, but *times have changed, and this survival mechanism may now be working against us.* Many of us find large amounts of stress in our everyday worlds because we consistently interpret parts of our lives as negative, and we believe that we have no control over them. In fact, some of us interpret nearly everything that happens during the day as negative and out of our control. Our nervous systems then react to these everyday situations essentially the same way the caveman's nervous system reacted to the chance meeting with a dangerous animal.

But when we encounter stressful situations on the highway (oh, how I dread those Los Angeles freeways at rush hour), we normally don't behave the way the caveman did when he encountered danger on the path. The caveman either ran away or stayed and fought the ancient enemy on the trail, and neither of these is a viable or safe option when you're behind the wheel on a multilane highway going seventy miles per hour.

As another example, you usually don't run away from or fight the office bully who constantly makes your life miserable. Although your breathing speeds up, blood pressure rises, heart rate increases, muscles tense, general metabolism rises, arteries spasm, and platelets are more likely to clump, you can't utilize the crisis mechanisms of battle or escape in the same ways your ancestors did. The modern version of battle or escape is much less physical and much less likely to be quickly resolved. It is long-term perceived stress, and your body responds long-term.

Modern life, with its tight schedules, rapid changes, diminishing family stability, constant negative news, emphasis on competition, and need for individuals to play multiple roles contains many situations that our bodies and brains interpret as negative and out of our control. And for most of those situations, the old flight-or-fight options don't fit.

We also seem to have more situations that lack closure and just seem to nag at us constantly. These are situations that can lead us to interpret large parts of our lives as stressful over long periods of time. With all this perceived stress comes the automatic crisis mechanisms described earlier. This means, however, that the bodily reactions of more rapid breathing, raised blood pressure, increased metabolism rate, higher heart rate, tensed muscles, arterial spasms, and platelet clumping are activated much more often and occur over much longer periods of time than they were designed for.

The problem is made all the greater because the body is responding to an anticipated physical response to stress rather than to the kinds of responses that we are socially and legally obligated to make today. Rather than be expended in a quick response to an immediate and short-lived physical situation, the body changes described above can become long-term contributors to such conditions as hypertension (high blood pressure), backaches, rashes, upset stomach, the inability to sleep or relax, muscle spasms, sore muscles, headaches, quick tempers, and higher probabilities of heart attacks and strokes. Thus, this fantastic short-term survival mechanism can easily become a long-term threat to our very survival if we don't understand it or don't use it properly. To counter that tendency, we will look at how we can apply some fundamental mental health concepts to this problem of dealing with stress.

Mental Health Strategies to Prevent, Reduce, Control and Use Stress

Stress is in your mind. You create or manufacture your stress through the ways in which you think. Here is a formula: **Events + Your Interpretation = Your Emotions.** For example, your boss doesn't make you feel stressed. He or she can only do or say things, such as finding fault with your work, assigning you a distasteful project, or giving unclear directions. You then interpret these words or actions as being stressful because you see them as negative and out of your control. These emotions and thoughts of stress trigger the ancestral escape-or-battle mechanism.

Consider the statement, "My boss is driving me crazy because he never says anything good about my work." You could just as well think, "It's too bad that my boss is so unobservant and doesn't recognize me for all the good work that I do, but I know how valuable I am, and I can live with that." In the same way, instead of thinking of unclear directions as putting more of a strain on you, you can consider them opportunities to be more creative in your work.

Remember, you can't have stress without your being at least partially responsible for it—because it's your interpretation of an event that generates the stress, not the event itself.

Everything is a possible source of stress. How you interpret any given situation determines how stressful it will be. Travel to a foreign country can be seen as a great opportunity to meet different and interesting people, or it can be seen as a fearful confrontation with unfamiliar and probably hostile people. A small, nonpoisonous snake can be seen as an attractive creature that has graceful movements, or it can be seen as a frightful reptile from which you must run. *If you allow yourself to be prone to stress, you can find some stress in just about anything.*

How you interpret any situation depends on your prior learning plus your belief system. For example, your parents and friends have taught you that a certain ethnic group is *"bad."* When you become lost and discover yourself in a neighborhood of this ethnic group, you're quite frightened. Your belief system thus has a tremendous impact on whether or not you view a given situation as stressful. If you've been taught that the world is essentially a bad place, you're more likely to interpret events and people as bad in some ways and, hence, more stressful to you.

Some kinds of tension can be good for you. When you find yourself in a real crisis situation that requires a fight-or-flight type of physical response (e.g., you're attacked by a mugger, you must escape from a burning building, you want to free someone who is pinned under a pile of rubble, and so on), you want the physiological reaction that you inherited from your caveman ancestors to be activated to give you the best chance possible of your or somebody else's survival.

You might also want to have a little normal, but well-controlled, tension to keep you on your toes when you're preparing for a game, speech, or other type of performance. When you feel that you have control of the situation, that the task is interesting, and that what you're doing is valuable, you won't trigger the flight-or-fight mechanism. You might allow yourself a few butterflies in the stomach or anticipatory tension, however, before the tennis match, speech, or play you're acting in. *Just keep your tensions and stresses short-term and controlled.* In fact, this is a good habit to follow any time you encounter a bad situation. View it as short-lived and within your control.

Control is perhaps the key factor in stressful situations.

In most cases, the more you feel you're in control the less the probability of stress. Conversely, the less you feel in control the more likely you are to experience stress. For example, you're less likely to be stressed if you're driving your car down a dangerous highway than if you're a passenger in an airplane, even though air travel has been proved to be a much safer means of transportation. Having control gives you more of a sense of security, which is the antithesis of stress.

Stress is brought about primarily by the way you think about things that happen to you—and since you can control your thoughts, then you can control your stress by how you think. In other words, if you can learn skills to control your thinking, you can increase your control over your stress. The best example of this is having a positive attitude. If you always look for the positive in any situation, you'll lessen the probability of stress, because stress thrives on the negative. *Any time you feel the symptoms of stress, do a quick check on your thinking about that situation, because the situation isn't causing the stress—your thinking is.*

Accept the fact that it's natural to have stressful situations in your life, and understand that you have control over how you react to them. For example, you know you're having headaches because you've overcommitted yourself and you feel your life is out of control. Therefore, you're now going to concentrate on the most important tasks and accept the fact that you'll have to do the less important tasks at a later time. If that doesn't work, you'll need to find someone else to complete some of the lesser tasks.

Avoid situations that have high potential for being stressful. Whenever possible, avoid the negative colleague, leave the unfulfilling job, ignore your obnoxious neighbor, transfer to a different department if your department has an unreasonable boss, or get rid of the car that keeps breaking down.

Nevertheless, you must carefully consider the long-term consequences of avoiding any given situation. Your primary goal must be to move toward a better situation. *The last thing you want is to leave a bad situation only to get yourself into a horrible one.*

Always look for the positive, even in negative situations. Think of your assets, count what you have left, and see the bright side. You may have lost some money, but you can earn that back— and you still have your health. When your idea didn't work, you didn't fail. You just learned another way *not* to do something. And you can celebrate the deceased person's life and move on just as easily as you can perpetually mourn his or her death.

Accept responsibility for any stress you experience. If your stress can't exist without your thinking it is stress, it has to be coming from inside you. Since *you* are largely responsible for your stress, it's not realistic for you to blame it on something outside you. Whether or not the situation is legitimately stressful, you're responsible for that interpretation. That's why you need to be careful when you interpret situations as stressful. When you hear yourself yelling, "I'm so stressed out about this!" you need to calm down and ask yourself, "Why am I letting myself get stressed? What can I do about it?"

Have some goals on which to focus your energy. *Stress can be the result of aimless activity.* For example, you might know you're doing a lot of work but you never seem to be getting anywhere. Other people seem to be passing you by, even though you're working as hard as or harder than they are. When you're not sure of the specific direction you want to take, you can become increasingly frustrated as you burn up energy going in circles. Have goals so you have a way to measure all your activity.

If you have too many goals, prioritize them and work only on the most important one(s). If possible, avoid taking on too many tasks, since stress can result from setting too many goals at once. If you believe you have to accomplish more things than time permits, you're putting yourself into a classic stressful situation. When you find this happening to you, take control of the situation by prioritizing what you need to do so you can concentrate your efforts on your most important goal or goals. That way you can use your finite time and energy in the most productive ways and feel good about it. In addition, it's usually good for your mental health to concentrate on a priority task, finish it, feel the satisfaction, celebrate, and then go on to the next highest priority.

Don't worry about the past. One of the most nonproductive things you can do is think about what you *should* have done and what you could have done. *The past is gone.* Certainly you should use your past experiences as lessons learned, but don't dwell on decisions or actions that didn't work out the way you would have preferred. You can't go back and do what you should have done, and you can't go back and *not* do what you shouldn't have done. If you feel you *must* mentally revisit the past, think about the events and people who made you feel good about your accomplishments and abilities.

Celebrate improvement rather than expect perfection. We all can improve, but no one can be perfect. If you accept only perfection as your standard, you automatically set yourself up for stress because you've set an impossible criterion. You can always be happier, but you probably will never be completely happy, at least not for long. You can avoid this kind of stress by striving to get incrementally better at what you are doing and feeling good about each improvement. Then repeat the process, again and again.

Expect success, but accept some setbacks as natural. Setbacks are normal, natural consequences of trying. Any time you undertake something, there's a possibility that it might not develop as you had anticipated. Even though you plan, work hard, visualize and expect success, you'll probably experience some setbacks. You can overcome them by having clear goals and by viewing your perceived failures as temporary inconveniences.

Never think of yourself as unsuccessful when you have a setback. A setback doesn't represent a permanent failure or permanent loss of control, and you shouldn't think of it as such. Maybe we shouldn't even allow the word *failure* into our thinking. Remember that any setback is only a temporary slowing of your progress and is your environment giving you feedback you can use later. The only real failure is to not try.

Work smarter, not harder. You cause yourself much frustration and distress when you try to solve problems by continuing to repeat an action that doesn't work rather than taking the time to find new perspectives and approaches. The guideline of "working smarter, not harder" isn't meant to discourage you from working hard. It does mean that if trying to beat down the brick wall with a hammer doesn't work, maybe it's time to see if there's a way around, under, or over it. Working smarter is also a lot more interesting and exciting than just working harder.

Accept responsibility for the use of your time. Don't say, "I didn't have the time." That kind of thinking says you've lost control of the time. Instead, say, "I didn't *take* the time." This statement puts you mentally in control and makes it obvious that you control your time. When you catch yourself saying, "I don't have the time to do something important," change it to "I will have to make the time" to do the important thing. This way you are choosing to use your time doing what you see as most important. When you deliberately prioritize the use of your time, you are controlling your time rather than having time control you.

Think in specifics. We often refer to "they," "the government," "the administration," "the bureaucracy," and other entities as sources of our stress. To your mind, these vague forces are difficult or impossible to control. You can become very frustrated because you can't talk to "them." "They" can't help you solve your problem. Such lack of closure to a problem can be a major source of potential stress. Therefore, instead of referring to "them" or some other generalized entity, be specific. A specific caused the problematic situation; a generality didn't. A specific is also needed to change it. For example, you might need to find Mr. Jones, the person who made the decision that's causing you problems. Mr. Jones can talk to you and discuss your problem. Mr. Jones might then introduce you to Ms. Smith, who can solve your problem. We have to find the specific people in the organization, not blame the organization. Be specific in your language and thoughts.

Be "in control" and choose, even when all your choices are undesirable. You always have the choice of doing something or not doing something; however, you might catch yourself saying something like, "He made me do it," which indicates that you don't see yourself in control of that part of your life. In this instance, you might be better off saying, "I chose to do it because the bad consequence of *not* doing it was even worse." In this case, you've taken control, and you've made a rational choice among undesirable alternatives rather than just accepting an inevitable, negative fate that was beyond your control. Thinking of yourself as "in control" not only can reduce your stress but also can better describe the reality that you *always* have some choices in every situation even if they are all bad ones.

Be careful how you describe yourself when you have less control than you'd like. Thinking of yourself as stressed can actually trigger your stress! Maybe you've referred to yourself as "stressed-out," "sick and tired" of something, "at the end of your rope" or "not able to take it anymore." Many people think to themselves like this, but such terms indicate that you have little or no control at that point, or that you are about to lose control if even one more negative thing were to happen. To feel in control, substitute phrases such as "temporarily inconvenient," "undesirable but controllable," and "unfortunate but getting better" in your self-talk as well as in your conversations with others. These terms show that you're in control of your life and that you interpret situations accordingly.

Don't allow yourself to get upset over rumors, hearsay, and other unreliable data. For example, some employees got very upset when they heard a rumor that their company was about to close. They worried about it at night, they discussed it among themselves, and kept building more stress as they speculated among themselves. Finally, after some days had gone by and the stress level was unbearable, one of them talked to management and learned there was no truth to the rumor. The distress they had caused themselves was completely unwarranted—and it wouldn't have happened had they just gotten the facts first rather than accepting the rumor without question. You can reduce stressful situations by dealing with facts and seeking reality.

Accept the fact that there are things over which you have no control. You may become upset about a famine in Africa even though it doesn't involve you in any direct way. You'll feel frustrated, too, because there's nothing you can directly do about it.

Note how the mass media increase your potential stress by delivering bad news such as this, over which you have no control. Watching, listening, and reading this constant flow of negativity can lead to stress, frustration, and cynicism if you let it. You could reduce the input of this negativity by ignoring the news.

However, if you're like many people, you probably want to stay informed. In that case, either do something to help rectify the negative situations you hear about (such as making a donation to assist the victims) or accept the fact that it's an event over which you have no control. Make a conscious decision and move on.

Be assertive when you feel you've been wronged. What do you do if a merchant sells you an inferior product? Do you keep the product, get angry, hate the merchant, never go back, and build up your stress? Or do you politely but firmly assert your right to a replacement or refund? *Being assertive is nothing more than diplomatically standing up for what you think is right.* Being assertive puts you more in control of your life and reduces the potential for stress.

Cultivate friends who have a positive outlook. Negative people can subtly influence your thinking toward negative thoughts if you allow them to do it. Avoid people who talk negatively about others, spread spiteful gossip, see the worst in every situation, and generally leave you feeling worse than before you met them. Try to surround yourself with positive people who enjoy life, find the best in people and situations, have a good sense of humor, and make you feel good about being alive.

Confront undesirable situations as soon as you can. A sure way to increase your stress is to put off dealing with an undesirable situation. While you're procrastinating, you're likely to imagine the situation to be much worse than it really is. Not doing something you know you need to do is almost always much worse than just doing what you need to do. Procrastination and stress go hand in hand. Aren't you always under more stress while you're procrastinating than when you're actually dealing with the situation?

Don't expect reciprocity. Some people become upset, frustrated or angry when they give a gift or do a favor and it's not reciprocated. Give a gift or favor just for the joy of giving, and enjoy the happiness of the recipient without expecting anything in return.

Don't make elephant droppings out of flyspecks. Some of us are quite good at taking what's really a small incident and thinking it into a major disaster. As a small incident, it was just an inconvenience. But when it's considered a disaster, it causes stress. For example, I have seen an accidental small scratch on someone's new car become a major incident that could have caused a fight resulting in an injury or death. Thoughts can manufacture catastrophes from small or insignificant happenings, so keep a sense of perspective. Don't let your thoughts make things worse than they really are.

Defuse stress with humor. Laughing at yourself or your circumstances can often be the quickest way to break tension and reduce the possibility of stress. Look for the ridiculous in a bad situation, since joking about it will probably make it less likely that you'll think of it in catastrophic terms. Humor defuses the caveman response of fight or flight. Sometimes a simple smile can defuse stress. Try it. Say, "I feel so stressed!" with a big smile and feel the stress disappear.

Reduce or discontinue stimulants. Most people find that they're tenser when they ingest large amounts of caffeine (typically found in coffee, regular tea, and cola drinks), nicotine and sugars. Again, moderation is important.

If you feel stressed, take a mental trip to a favorite spot, or mentally do something you find especially enjoyable. For feelings of tension and stress, substitute thoughts of you in a favorite place or doing a favorite activity. Possibilities include envisioning such things as the seashore, a forest or cathedral, or activities like sailing, playing ball or fishing—whatever you find calming.

If you feel stressed, do some relaxation exercises or meditate. There are many types of relaxation exercises, and you should try several to find out if some work for you. One of the most popular methods is to tense your muscles and then relax them, individually, beginning at your feet and gradually working your way up to your head, repeating until your whole body is relaxed.

Meditation is a simple and effective way to reduce stress and refresh oneself. If you don't know how, you can take a class or use a recording as a guide. Scientific studies suggest that meditation is effective for reducing stress. If it takes your thoughts off stress, you have reduced the stress, right?

Regular exercise is a good way to both prevent and treat stress. Walking, jogging, swimming, biking, and other exercises during which the heart rate is moderately elevated for a period of time are valuable when dealing with stress. They are also excellent for strengthening the cardiovascular system. Any exercise is better than none, but aerobic exercise four or five times a week for at least thirty minutes per session is generally accepted as a good compromise between time expended and benefits derived. See the chapter on physical health for a much more comprehensive discussion.

Make a decision and then enjoy it. Many people have the habit of making a decision and then, almost immediately, starting to second-guess themselves. Second-guessing and doubting build unnecessary stress. If you buy a white car, enjoy it and don't think you should have purchased the red one. Enjoy the benefits resulting from your well-researched decisions rather than increase your inner turmoil by continuing to debate alternatives after you've already made the decision.

Recognize the fact that almost any change will bring a greater-than-normal potential for stress. Changes in your life, even those that are mostly positive, can cause anxiety and stress if you allow them to. Change involves the uneasiness of breaking comfortable patterns and entering the unknown. It's natural to have some stressful feelings when you experience something unfamiliar, so accept those feelings as natural and then look for the stimulation and excitement of exploring new territory. Change is a chance to grow, and you can't grow without changing. Change doesn't have to be stressful; whether or not it's stressful will be primarily the result of your thinking.

Ask yourself, "How important is it?" When you feel the signs of stress coming on (mine is a tightening neck), ask yourself, "Just how important is this?" This simple question is what I use to give myself perspective. Without asking that question about some of our life setbacks, we can easily make a big deal out of what is a little inconvenience.

Think of problems as opportunities. You can reduce tension and stress by thinking of negative situations as opportunities to see new prospects, creatively solve problems, and develop positives out of negatives. For example, the theft of a tool you use for work could become an opportunity to invent a new tool or to purchase a more efficient one.

Accept the fact that not everyone will like you or like what you do. You can eliminate a lot of potential stress from your life if you keep in mind that you'll never be able to please everybody. Human beings come with too many varieties of values and outlooks for you to expect to please them all. Trying to please all of your potential critics is a sure way to increase your stress. A very wise person has said, "What you think of me is none of my business." Makes sense to me in most cases.

Do your best and feel good about it, even if it isn't perfect. Set high standards for yourself, but make sure those standards are realistic. Being a perfectionist is not realistic. No one is perfect, at least not for long. However, it *is* realistic to put your best effort into achieving your goals. If you do your best at something, you can be satisfied with yourself. You've used as much of your potential as you can at the time, and neither you nor anyone else can expect more than that. If something isn't worth your best effort, then it probably isn't worth doing in the first place.

Understand that all choices involve some kind of tradeoff. Every time you choose one thing, you have to give up something else. If you don't understand tradeoffs, you can be an unhappy and tense person who is always looking for the one-hundred-percent-fail-proof, completely correct answer or decision. Since such a perfect guarantee doesn't exist, you're setting yourself up for an endless, fruitless, and frustrating search. Analyze the tradeoffs in any decision-making situation, make your choice, accept the things you have to forego, and then enjoy your choice.

Accept the fact that people aren't likely to change in the ways you want. Trying to get someone else to change to meet your expectations is a frustrating situation with high potential as a stressful situation. Others change when they see the need to change, not when you see it. Attempting to force someone to change when he or she doesn't want to can become especially stressful for everyone involved.

Get rid of the clutter in your life. Messy houses, garages, closets, offices, desks, cars, and so on are potential sources of stress because they represent constant reminders of things you need to get done. They nag at you whenever you see them. Tidy up these physical things in your life and see if you don't feel more relaxed—because you automatically tidied up your mind in the process.

Complete your unfinished relationship business. This includes any relationships or dealings with people or organizations that are now at an uncomfortable stage. Apologize to your sister for the angry things you said. Finally send the thank-you letter to someone who did you a favor. Send a note of praise to the dedicated principal or teacher who is doing such a great job with your child. You might think of cleaning up your relationships much the same way as you would clean up the physical clutter in your life. As you overcome procrastination and bring closure to this unfinished human relationship business, you'll reduce much potential stress.

Be consistent in your beliefs and actions. If you choose to behave in ways that are inconsistent with what you profess, you're creating situations with high potential for stress. Doing something you know is wrong creates a form of self-dishonesty or hypocrisy. Any sane person will feel tension when knowingly behaving in ways that are incongruent with a professed belief system. In those instances, you know you are a hypocrite. Actually, you *do* behave consistently with what you believe is best for you at any given time. However, the belief you *profess* might be different.

Determine when to stop. You can create a stressful situation when you don't realize you're overdoing something. For example, a student kept going to the library "just one more time" to get additional sources for a term paper that was due in just two more days. Without a single word written at that point, he had to cut classes and go without sleep to get the paper in on time. He had created a very stressful situation for himself, since he should have been writing rather than overdoing his search for source material. Know when to stop.

Consider setting realistic limits as guides for knowing when to stop. For example, set a dollar amount below which you will no longer bother to comparison-shop. Say you choose $50. After establishing that figure, you will comparison-shop only for items more expensive than the limit you've set. This will save you a lot of time and hassle.

Choose a career you love. When you choose your vocation, choose something you really love to do if you possibly can. Certainly you should consider the income factor, but the happiest and most stress-resistant people are those who really love their work. It seems that it's easier to adjust one's economic lifestyle lower than it is to find interesting, exciting, and fulfilling work. The theory is that when you find a vocation to which you can be highly committed, you will probably do it well and make a reasonable living as a result. But there's no guarantee.

Don't compare yourself with others. It's very easy to create a potentially stressful situation when you compare yourself with those who seem to be the richest, most famous, most talented, most attractive, and happiest people. If you must compare yourself, compare yourself with someone who has less than you. But it's probably best not to compare yourself with anyone else at all. What purpose does it serve? Be proud of who you are and what you contribute.

Add variety to your life. Doing the same thing for too long

66

can cause stress. This is a form of burnout, usually characterized by feelings of boredom and lack of challenge. The stimulation of adventure, discovery, and problem solving has been lost, and everything feels the same. Adding variety and change to your life can lessen this feeling of constant sameness, often described as "being in a rut." With a bit of effort, you can add variety to any area of your life, from what food you eat to what vacation you choose, from the way you do your job to the route you take to and from that work.

Look for what you have left, not for what you've lost. Negative thinking can cause stress, so if you consciously look for positives in every phase of your life, you'll find that you have less stress. You certainly can't overlook negative life events, because you have to deal with them and you can also learn from them. Still, there are always some positive aspects in any situation if you change your perspective from negative to positive. When you focus on the positives of a bad situation, you're identifying what you have left to work with. It does no good whatsoever to focus on what was lost. For example, if your house were to burn down, would you bemoan what was lost or be thankful for the people and possessions that survived? What survived is now what you possess, control, and can use to build your future. Seeing the bright side is seeing the right side, as far as stress is concerned.

Consider dropping the word "stress" from your vocabulary. Stress has come to mean being caught in a very strong, negative situation over which you have no control. So if you use *stress* to describe your mental and physical state, you're telling your mind that you're not in control of a negative situation. Simply thinking about being in a stressful situation can trigger the run-or-fight mechanism, but thinking about being in an "unfortunate situation" or about being "temporarily inconvenienced" should not trigger this reaction. You might want to find a substitute for the term "stressed" that would have less of a frenzied, out-of-control connotation to you. Terms such as "concerned" or "perplexed" can connote a mental condition that is more internally controlled and oriented toward being a problem that can be solved. I personally like to say that "my environment has just given me some negative feedback and I need to look into it." How you talk to yourself can make a big difference!

Mind as Tool

Our minds are our most important tools. If we know better how our minds work, we can use them more efficiently for our benefit. Our minds contain our thoughts. Ultimately, we are our physical bodies and our thoughts. Having good mental health involves using our thoughts in constructive ways and recognizing destructive thinking so we can avoid it. What we think about leads to our actions, and our actions have consequences for ourselves, for others, and for our environment. We owe it to ourselves, others, and the environment to learn more about gaining and maintaining optimal mental health.

Below you will find some key words and phrases that will aid you in further pursuing knowledge about thought and its uses. Invest some time in yourself and investigate some of the following:

- Happiness.
- Habits.
- Assertiveness.
- Emotions.
- Self-esteem.
- Self-control.
- Humor.
- Boomerang theory.
- Worry.
- Values and beliefs -> behavior -> consequences.
- Motivation.
- Success.
- Journeys and destinations.
- Past, present, future outlooks.

- Mind as filter.

- Stress.

- Positive versus negative thinking.

- Self-talk.

- Realistic optimism.

- Procrastination.

- Mass media influences.

- You are ultimately responsible.

- Affirmations.

- Guided imagery.

- Change or accept unchangeable.

- Love.

- IQ and other mental tests.

- Others' judgment of you.

- Entertainment trap.

- Fulfillment.

- Control continuum.

- Self-concept, self-image.

- Creativity.

- First impressions.

- "I choose to" versus "I have to."

- Selective forgetting.

- Making changes.

- "That's just the way I am."

- What we think about tends to come about.

FACTOR 3

Gaining and Maintaining Financial Security

Why are some people financially secure and comfortable while other people are under constant stress to obtain the bare necessities of life? What do these wealthier people do that poorer people don't do? How can someone who is very rich be unhappy and how can someone who is poorer be happy? What lessons can we learn from examining the actions of both those who are financially secure and those not so secure?

Financially secure people might have had some lucky breaks or even an inheritance to help them along, but much of people's wealth comes from a combination of knowledge, planning, work, and consistent habits over a long period of time. You can gain ideas here about how to increase your wealth to the point of financial security, but you will have to take the responsibility for consistently practicing those ideas.

Before I elaborate on what you might do, let's look at a list of common economic behaviors that will undermine your financial future. Do any of these describe you?

1. Buy a new car every two years or whenever you think you need to upgrade your image. Put as little down as possible and stretch the payments out as far as you can.

2. Purchase designer clothes and other expensive name-brand merchandise because creating an impression is really important to you and you want to fit into your group.

3. Never wait to buy something. Buy it on credit and pay the purchase price plus the interest. Never compute the total cost.

4. Eat out as often as possible and patronize expensive restaurants. Don't consider saving all that additional monthly cost by simply cooking and eating at home, where you also could eat healthier.

5. Don't establish a crisis fund. If your transmission fails, the central air conditioning condenser needs replacing, or the dentist says you need new bridgework, just charge it.

6. Spend all your free time watching television, keeping up with the latest sports news, playing video games, surfing the Internet or texting. Don't educate yourself about finance because you think it's really boring and unpleasant subject.

7. Don't save money when you're young, since you've got plenty of time to do that later. Saving is for older people.

8. Don't bother balancing your checkbook. The bank will let you know if there's a problem.

9. Always buy the very latest model of cell phones, tablets, and other electronic gadgets so you can pay the full or premium price.

10. Buy the largest, most elaborate house you can find and make sure it's in the trendiest neighborhood. Don't forget to add a pool. Don't take maintenance, taxes, utilities, and the many other expenses into account.

11. Never miss an opportunity to acquire another charge card. The more you have, the more stuff you can buy.

12. Uncritically watch advertisements and commercials. They're great guides on how to spend your money.

13. If you ever come into some extra money, be sure to use all of it immediately to buy what you really, really want. If you want an expensive car and your extra money isn't enough to purchase it, use the new money as a down payment.

14. Don't try to distinguish between your "needs" and your "wants." If you want it, buy it.

15. Do everything necessary to "keep up with your

neighbors." Wow, see that new car in their driveway?

16. Only the best stuff is good enough for you. Don't be selfish; also buy the most expensive gifts for your family and friends. That way you know they will love you.

17. Never consider spending less. Only think about where and how you can get more money.

18. Buy strictly for an item's price and looks. Forget quality, durability, repair record, safety, and other factors that will contribute to its ultimate cost.

19. Don't create a financial plan. You have better things to do right now, like entertaining yourself.

20. Don't concern yourself with the difference between assets and liabilities.

21. Buy large, expensive, pedigreed, high-maintenance pets.

22. Even if you can't afford it, always hire someone to do work you don't want to do or don't want to take the time to do.

23. Tell yourself that when you buy the next expensive gadget everyone's been talking about, you'll finally be happy.

24. Even if you think it sounds too good to be true, buy it or invest in it.

Hopefully, not many of those self-sabotaging behaviors describe you. If they do, please consider doing something about them.

Behaviors of People Who Are Gaining and Maintaining Wealth

I assume that you would like to be wealthy, or at least wealthier. When I did research into wealth, I studied what wealthy people tend to do that poorer people tend not to do. Of course, the opposite is also something to study. What do poorer people do that wealthier people do not do? See the examples above. OK, how do most people who are wealthy get that way?

Are financially secure, wealthy people smarter than everyone else? Are they just luckier than most? Or did they somehow manage to pull off an elaborate scheme of some kind and not get caught?

In most cases, the answer is "none of the above."

Contrary to what Hollywood would have you believe, wealth is most often the result of hard work, applied knowledge and careful planning. And while inheriting money, winning the lottery, or perpetrating a Wall Street scam can quickly make you rich, suddenly acquired wealth seldom occurs in the real world. Even if you did defy the unbelievable odds and won a large lottery, you would probably learn that this quick money can evaporate just as quickly *if you're unprepared for the responsibility of managing it.*

If you never hold the winning Powerball ticket or never learn you're sole heir to the fortune left by your eccentric uncle, you shouldn't necessarily feel bad about it. Studies of lottery winners and those who inherit large fortunes show that they're very likely to lose or squander their newfound wealth because they were unprepared to manage the money and did not research how they could manage it.

For example, on my first job as a teenager in a steel plant in Kansas City, I met a coworker who had been injured in the plant several years ago. A bundle of steel rods had hit him in the head and badly disfigured his face. The company settled with him for a substantial sum. He promptly quit his job, bought a huge expensive new home, bought a top-of-the-line expensive new car, and proceeded to sit home and drink cases of beer a day. In a few years he had lost the house and his car and had done considerable damage to his health. When I met him he was back at the same plant, less healthy and with a disfigured face, doing the same work and getting the same pay. He will always remain to me a most vivid example of the old saying "Easy come, easy go." Because you have money doesn't mean that you can manage it.

When you study what financially secure people *do* that financially insecure people *don't do,* you will find that their methods are simple, logical, and consistently applied. If they can take these steps, you can, too. No matter what your current financial position is, you need to start a plan *now* that includes what wealthy people do. You also deserve to feel more secure, to have more peace of mind, and to have increased purchasing power and a wider range of choices just like they do.

What's more, you'll be more likely to hang onto your wealth once you've achieved it. Wealthy people typically gain wealth through discipline, persistence, knowledge, work, and intensity of focus, and they use those same attributes when managing their assets.

That said, what are some of the basic, specific steps that the vast majority of wealthy people use to accumulate wealth in their consistent, informed, long-term, planned and methodical way?

Step 1: Live Below Your Means

This step is very straightforward and easy to understand. I can't believe that I need to list it. No matter what your income, you must spend less than that amount, week after week, month after month, and year after year. Your income must *consistently* exceed your outgo. That is a simple math problem even for a second grader.

But what do you do if you are spending more than you make? First, maybe go back to the second grade and brush up on your subtraction skills.

As a rule of thumb, it's almost always easier to cut spending than to increase income. You can start by determining what specific things you are purchasing. Next, you need to determine which of the things you purchase are things you *need* and which are things you just *want*. Take eating, for example. This is a large item in anyone's budget. But while most people would agree that eating adequate nutritious food is a necessity, they would also agree that eating out at a restaurant is almost always more expensive and generally less healthy. While we *need* nutritious food to live and be physically healthy, eating out is something we don't need to do. We just *want* to do it.

Of course, to make up for the expense of eating out a lot, you *could* find ways to increase your income, like working overtime or getting a second job. But wouldn't it make more sense to cut way down on restaurant tabs or just eliminate them entirely except for very special occasions? You can learn to cook if you don't know how. And by learning to cook and choosing more nutritious ingredients, you can be healthier in addition to saving money.

People are also often very surprised when they keep track of both their spontaneous purchases and their habitual purchases of what they eat and drink between regular meals. Do you know how much you spend every week on soda and energy drinks, expensive coffees, crackers, cakes, candy bars, and other snack foods of all kinds? A lot of those seemingly small expenses add up to large sums over time, and most of those kinds of purchases are full of empty calories that add up to bad health. By usually eating the food you need at home and shopping more carefully, you can significantly reduce your expenditure for food. What's more, you can also cut down on calories, learn new skills, and improve your health in the process.

Now, besides food, what other physical things and services do you really *need* in your life? Most people all over the world pursue common human needs of food, clean water, adequate sleep, companionship, moderate exercise, medical and dental care, a safe place to call home, and a way to make a living. These are common needs that are satisfied in many different ways.

Most people in the world are struggling to just stay alive at a basic-needs level. They can find much of their happiness when they find enough food and get some shelter. However, many of us, especially in the industrialized world, satisfy our basic needs relatively easily and take them for granted. We then often fall into the trap of thinking that what will make us happy is when we get stuff we want. Some of us have begun to say we can't be happy unless we have a late-model car, live in a certain house or neighborhood, wear name-brand clothes, or play golf three times a week. Others crave international travel, wilderness excursions, or the ability to enjoy expensive sports and activities like polo, auto racing, or flying their own airplane. Our wants can begin to be thought of as our needs. We can be led by advertising and group pressure to believe the more wants we can satisfy the happier and more fulfilled we will be.

Although we think we'll be happier after obtaining the new item or experience, we're usually not, at least not for long. The novelty wears off after a few days or weeks and soon we want something else that is newer, bigger, more "prestigious," or more impressive to others. A couple of examples:

Jerry finally bought the luxury car of his dreams, but a few months later he spots a new sports car and wonders if he should have bought a sports car instead. Now he says he won't be happy until he has one of each.

An acquaintance and his family had a nice home that fit them well. They were happy until many other couples they knew were buying new, very large, and more attractive homes. So they also bought one of these huge homes so they would be happier. After making their move, they discovered that the bigger home carried with it expenses and upkeep they hadn't considered. The economic pressures and stress caused by owning a house much bigger than they needed began affecting their stress levels and were causing them to argue about money. They eventually realized that they simply were not living within their means and would be much happier when they bought a home they could easily afford.

Be realistic about which of your expenditures are for actual needs and which are merely for "wants." As an initial goal, try cutting your "want" category spending by at least half. Experiment to get a reasonable amount for you. This saved money can then be used to work toward your future financial security.

Step 2: Start a Savings Plan—Pay Your Future First and Then Live on the Rest

You have developed the habit of conscious buying and are now being careful to purchase goods and services that you need and few frivolous things that you want. The next step is to develop the habit of formal, consistent saving. By this I mean that you deliberately put money aside as savings from your income as the first thing you do when you are paid.

For example, say you work for an employer and you get paid a salary each two weeks. If your employer has the ability to do so, have him deduct a certain amount from your paycheck to be put into a savings account that you have set up. It works just like the federal, state, and social security taxes that are deducted from your check. After your savings are deducted, then you budget the rest of your salary for you to live on. If your employer can't deduct the savings automatically or if you own your own business, you can work out some automatic system of building a savings account. You never see the money you are saving and you learn to live on what you have left.

You can also do a simple thing like utilizing an employer's 401(k) option and contribute into it up to the maximum of any matching funds that are available to add to savings. Check with your employer.

Don't fall into the trap that most people do. That trap is the reverse of saving first. These folks say they will live off the money in their paychecks and then, if any money is left, they will save it. How well do you think that works? How many times has that worked for you or for others you know? I have never heard anyone tell me that they had money left over last month and they put it in their savings account. *Save first and live off the rest.*

When we were first married, my wife and I saved money by putting about fifteen percent of our paychecks directly into a savings account and watched it grow. We lived in a small but adequate trailer, had a good but older car, and very seldom ate out. We worked and studied for our future rather than using our money for expensive entertainment. We learned to enjoy simple pleasures in life rather than spend our money on luxuries that would soon lose their luster. We were happy with our life on the lesser amount of money we had left after saving up front. We simply adjusted our lifestyle to fit our means. It wasn't hard. Plus, we had the security of knowing we had money in the bank if we had an emergency. That is when I first realized the meaning of the saying that "the poor man's catastrophe is the rich man's inconvenience."

Even after you have saved a substantial amount, you want to continue to pay your future first as long as you are receiving an income. We are living longer. Living will probably get more expensive. You probably will want to have more unique experiences in the future. *For these and many more reasons I hope you will want to maximize your savings as much as possible, as long as possible, as consistently as possible.* You can have a great life and still continue to save first.

Step 3: Create an Emergency or Crisis Fund

Most people call this an emergency fund. But *crisis fund* may be a better term for it. (From a psychological standpoint, you might be less likely to raid a crisis fund.) But call it what you like, you need money specifically set aside for unforeseen setbacks. As an initial goal, strive to accumulate at least $1,000 for this purpose. Then add to that amount as often as you can until you have enough funds in reserve to cover several months of living expenses. Most financial-planning literature says three to six months' expenses need to be covered, but your personal circumstances will determine what you should save. I personally would err on the safe side.

Remember, not many things in life qualify as an authentic crisis. They include such events as health emergencies, a sudden drop in income due to unexpected unemployment or the inability to work after an illness or accident, major car repairs, broken water pipes in your house, illness of a family member, stolen property, or a family member or neighbor who needs temporary help.

No matter how much you might be yearning to own the latest smartphone, tablet, laptop or digital camera, it does not qualify as a crisis. Joining a friend on a luxury cruise does not constitute a crisis. Getting your spouse or child a new car does not constitute a crisis. Of course, none of these things qualify as crises, even to make someone else happy—but you'd be surprised how many people rationalize raiding their crisis funds for superficial purposes.

Establishing and using reserves strictly for emergencies will test your willpower and ability to delay gratification. All that money is just sitting there tempting you to use it. It has to be in a fund that is liquid (easily accessible) so you can get to it when you unexpectedly need it. It will just be sitting there waiting to be used. It might tempt you every time you think about it. It will test you and test you again, but you have the willpower to resist and delay that urge for instant gratification.

If you think about it, the best thing would be for your crisis fund to never be used, not one penny of it.

Step 4: Do You Need Insurance?

This is a simple but necessary step to consider. What kinds of insurance do you need in your personal situation? Here are the questions you need to ask yourself.

1. Does anyone have to depend on my income if I should die? In most cases, term life insurance is your best way to go.

2. What would happen to me and others if I were sick for a few days or weeks? This is your health insurance or short-term disability insurance.

3. What would happen to me and others if I were to be permanently disabled or would lose income with a long-term disability of months or years? This is long-term disability insurance.

4. What if someone got hurt in my home or apartment? What if my home or furnishings burned, were damaged, or were stolen? Homeowners insurance comes in several packages, so you need to choose carefully. Even if you live in an apartment, you need to consider some liability insurance and contents insurance.

5. Do I have adequate insurance coverage on my auto, motorcycle, and "toys" that might injure others or me? Your state will probably require you to have insurance on vehicles, but be sure that you can cover damage and injuries that might result even from recreational vehicles.

It is crucial that you find an insurance company and an agent you can trust. Consult friends, the Better Business Bureau, your state's insurance regulator, consumer agencies, and other advocacy agencies to find agents you want to interview. When you choose an agent and a company you feel comfortable with, I suggest that you consider getting all your insurances in that one place if you can.

That way you have some leverage in the event there is a problem.

I learned this from experience. While I was fully stopped at an intersection, a car hit me from behind but then left the scene before I could get any identification of the driver or car. The police verified that the driver who rear-ended my stopped car was completely at fault. After the insurance company had my car repaired, the company notified me that it was raising my rates. Since I was in no way at fault, I informed the insurance company that I would cancel all seven of my policies I currently had with them, if they raised the rates on my car. My original rate was quietly restored. That is what I mean by getting leverage with your insurance carrier, and how it can be used to your advantage.

Step 5: If You Have to Buy Something on Credit, You Can't Afford It

Wealthy people don't pay interest, they collect interest. When you buy something on credit, you are paying the lender extra money, often substantial, for the privilege of buying your purchase before you can afford it. If you could afford it, you would pay cash. If you saved money for the purchase and then bought it for cash, you would save paying interest and you might be able to negotiate a better price because you are paying cash.

You want to be accumulating wealth. But if you are paying interest, you are just helping someone else accumulate wealth. Month after month, year after year, you are contributing your interest payments to someone else's financial security when you could be contributing those sums to secure your own financial future. Starting now, with a few possible exceptions, do yourself a favor and stop buying things on time.

If that seems like a hard reality to swallow, remember that although you won't be able to afford some of the things you want *right now*, you will probably be able to afford them in the future. After all, the whole idea of becoming wealthy is to acquire a comfortable lifestyle, one that includes most, if not all, of the things you can't afford today. But first you'll need to build wealth, and a major key to building wealth is to avoid the interest trap posed by credit cards and installment plans.

If you already have a number of credit card balances and installment loans, make a plan for paying those balances off as quickly as possible. To get started, take some of that money you have saved by using some of the previous suggestions made in this chapter for reducing your spending, and use what you save to pay down debt. But that might not be enough. To make significant headway, you may also need to take a second job or devise other ways to increase your income temporarily. Whatever you need to do to eliminate existing debt, start doing it now.

Here are two approaches I have seen that were used successfully to pay down credit card debt. The first, which seems most logical to me, is to concentrate on paying off the credit card debt that has the highest interest rate and then pay off the next highest until all are paid off.

The other approach is to pay off the smallest debt first regardless of the interest rate, and then pay off the next smallest until they are all eliminated. The psychology behind this approach is that getting the easiest one paid off will foster a sense of accomplishment and give you momentum to continue. I could see someone starting with the smallest debt to get started and gain momentum. Then go after the highest-interest loans. Whatever way you do it, you will feel a great deal of accomplishment, and a major source of the stress in your life will be eliminated.

The average American family owes well over $15,000 in credit card debt. If yours is one of these families, consider this: By making only minimum monthly payments, you will take twenty-nine years to pay that debt in full. That's provided you make at least minimum payments each and every month to avoid penalties and even higher interest rates. And it assumes that you use your head and do the obvious thing by not putting additional items and services on that card in the meantime.

The same average family has one or more cars in its driveway or garage that were purchased on installment plans of up to six years. The high interest on those loans represents a large percentage of the total cost the family is paying for each vehicle. If this fits you, go check your statements and determine how much you actually will pay for that car or cars in total.

Between the high interest paid on credit card balances and

the interest paid on auto loans, this average family—a family deeply in debt—is wasting thousands of dollars annually. And since this is the very money they could be saving and investing to build wealth over time, the family is squandering its opportunity to become affluent and have the luxury of more life choices and the lessening of the inevitable stresses of always "just getting by."

Now destroy all your credit cards except your favorite one. There are a few reasonable situations when you can use that one credit card or buy on installment plans. Here are those legitimate uses:

- Buying a home mortgage, when you can reasonably expect significant appreciation in the home's value during the time you will live in it. That is, you believe that your home is not only a great place to live but is also an asset that has a good chance to gain value in the long run. However, there are many pros and cons of home ownership versus renting. Variables such as income, family size, job stability, possible relocation, cost of housing, and the area's cost of living need to be considered. In America, we have generally accepted that owning a house is almost always good, but renting should be considered as a viable alternative—it has many advantages if you objectively compare them. Carefully calculate the costs and benefits of a home purchase, which is likely to be the largest you'll ever make.

- Purchasing items or services for which you are allowed to pay the balance in full within a short time (say ninety days) without owing any interest. These are often called same-as-cash purchases.

- Making purchases on credit cards for one or more attached advantages (known as perks), *but only when you know you will pay the balance off in full within thirty days.* Worthwhile perks can include purchase protection, extended warranties, cash, rewards points you can put toward other items or services, and others. Just be sure you can—and will—pay the balance in full at the end of the month, before any interest is added! This is what I do.

I have never paid a cent in interest over many decades, but I have enjoyed the convenience of not carrying cash and have redeemed thousands of dollars in rewards. This is one of those things in life that seems too good to be true, but it really is!

- Obtaining an item or service of absolutely vital importance to your health or safety or someone else's. Note that if you plan your finances correctly and establish a crisis fund for this type of emergency, this should rarely happen unless the crisis is catastrophic or you don't have enough for emergencies. A large crisis fund and proper insurance should lessen the probability of your having to use this alternative.

What if, after reading about the obvious disadvantages of paying interest and absorbing everything else in this book, you still succumb to the temptation of buying on credit?

If you can't stop charging, you don't have the willpower to acquire wealth. You may as well say goodbye to your future financial security right now. To accumulate wealth, beyond the four possible exceptions mentioned above, you must pay up front for the products and services you want or go without them until you can.

If there is another way, let me and the rest of the world know.

Step 6: Learn to Delay Gratification

The inability to delay gratification is one of the major roots of financial evils. When people spend more than they make, a primary cause is that they can't delay their gratification until they have made enough to buy the product or service they desire. Savings plans are sabotaged by people's lack of restraint when it comes to stuff they think they must have *now*. Crisis funds are not funded because there is always something new or bigger or more impressive that we must have now. Most purchases made on credit cards or installment plans are made because someone wants something right now. The attitude is, "Why should I wait to have something tomorrow—or next year—when I can have it today?"

This type of thinking means the advertising agencies have done their job well. Advertisements are based on very sophisticated research models that work on the soft spots of those of us who can't delay our gratification. Commercials tell us that products will make us more attractive, especially to members of the opposite sex. They have us believe that their products will make us look younger. We are told that their products will attract us new friends. We are told that this new pill will take away pain, melt off fat, increase muscle, grow hair or make us smell better. They also know that if they repeat those claims enough and we hear them often enough, we are more likely to buy their products or services. They can be so successful with their advertising that we can begin to think of our wants as being needs ... immediate needs. What kind of advertising is most likely to get you to want instant gratification?

Now add salesmanship and specific marketing to the mix. We get softened up by the advertisements aimed at triggering one set of emotions, and then we are further induced to purchase the product because the product is *on sale* or it is the *new model* that has just been introduced and updated. Notice how many products have frequent minor changes to catch those people who must have the latest, especially when it relates to technology such as all the variations on cell phones. Some people are so taken in by the commercial propaganda that they actually camp out for days in order to purchase the very first phones. Those new products are usually purchased at a full or premium price. Lemmings don't follow each other and really jump off cliffs like we used to believe, but many of us go where the advertisers lead us as if we were those little creatures behaving as the myth said they would.

What is it that makes delaying gratification so difficult? It is the same thing that makes changing habits difficult. It is the same thing that makes prevention easy to overlook while we are looking for cures. Instant gratification is immediate satisfaction. Delayed gratification means our satisfaction is in the future. We want to be happy now. It is natural to act that way. Think about it. We humans are wired to want instant gratification. Perhaps you remember those studies where children were asked whether they would rather have one cookie today or wait until a later time to get several cookies. The vast majority of the kids take the one cookie right now. Not until their brains further mature are they able to see that delaying gratification is actually the best choice if they want to gather cookies, which would be a kind of wealth to them. It seems that some of us never get out of the one-cookie-now stage.

Why do some people continue to smoke cigarettes despite overwhelming evidence that it is probably the worst thing you can do to your health? And they do it voluntarily. The smoking of a cigarette gives them instant gratification. They look forward to it. They get a temporary *lift* from it. What about the dangers? What about all the damage they are doing to their bodies? Don't they want good health? Sure, they want good health. But the short-term instant gratification they get from the cigarette overrides the long-term benefits of good health.

"Now" trumps "future" unless we take the time to objectively look at the situation we are in and calculate the costs and benefits (gratifications) in the long run instead of just the short run. Those of us who continue to make economic decisions based on our instant gratification have to take the time to research and apply proven methods of attaining and maintaining wealth. Otherwise, our behaviors based on short-term instant gratification can lead us to long-term lives of financial distress and ultimate ruin.

Step 7: Think About Your Retirement

First, you and any significant other in your life need to discuss what you mean by retirement. What mental picture do you get when you visualize yourself retired? Are you in a rocking chair on the front porch sipping your favorite drink? Are you sitting in your recliner watching television? Maybe you are playing golf. Maybe you are on a cruise boat or on a trip to see the sights of someplace you have never been. Maybe you have joined the Peace Corps or are helping scientists on a working vacation. Maybe you are building houses in Cambodia. Maybe you are volunteering as a docent in a museum, as a park ranger, at a food bank, or with homeless children. These are just some of the endless possibilities open to you if you retire.

I really don't want you to use the usual definition of the term *retirement*. It connotes too much of the rocking chair, recliner, napping, escapism, passive, entertain-myself-until-I-die existence. I prefer to think of what we call retirement as "a change in meaningful activity." Let's look at this phrase. When you "change," you terminate or withdraw from your normal working life. You now have the opportunity to do something else.

"Meaningful activity" means you need to stay active doing something you see as meaningful and rewarding. Let me apply that phrase to the five factors cited in this book. Meaningful activity would be doing activities that promote your (1) physical health, (2) mental health, and (3) financial security. You can continue to hone and use your (4) skills of problem solving and critical thinking. You can model acts of (5) responsibility to others, the environment, and yourself. You can be active and useful as well as enjoy a more relaxed lifestyle.

You are keeping your physical health by enjoying preparing and eating a variety of healthy real foods and enjoying a variety of moderate exercise activities. You are keeping your mind healthy by having a variety of experiences that involve problem-solving, producing things, being creative, and being interactive. You are monitoring your finances and continuing to read about and develop strategies to make your money work for you. You are constantly learning new skills and strategies and applying them to all facets of your life.

You do no harm to others, the environment or yourself, and you look for ways to enhance the lives of others, to improve the environment, and to give yourself the respect you deserve.

I am not going into the specifics of how you accumulate wealth for retirement other than what I've said in the other sections of this chapter and this: Start as early as possible, and save as much and as consistently as possible. As you are starting your saving plan, start familiarizing yourself with the vocabulary of financial planning. Carefully choose and vet a financial planner. Use the list of key terms at the end of the chapter to begin your research of planning your personal financial strategies. Listen to financial planners on the radio, attend free seminars, talk to wealthy people, and generally keep your eyes and ears open to information. Make informed decisions. You must take ultimate responsibility for your decisions.

Approaches to Retirement

I think there are at least three different approaches we can choose from as we prepare for retirement.

The first is to *just keep working*. If you enjoy what you are doing and you are doing work that is meaningful and fulfilling, why stop? It is one thing to be terminated for some reason, but why self-terminate because of some tradition that around a certain age most Americans believe they should expect to retire? Most people don't question the idea that they should retire. In fact, most people want to retire as early as possible. They haven't really thought about it, but intuitively it seems to be what they should strive for. Often they give up jobs they enjoy in order to retire early *because that's what everybody does*. Then they find retirement boring, miss their colleagues, miss the mental stimulation, miss the problem-solving in their old job, and maybe make their spouses' lives miserable. They often also discover that they have retired too soon and do not have enough money saved. If your job is fulfilling, consider staying in it as long as you can. Another alternative would be to stay in your job as long as you can but do it part time. That way you still have some income, you have work you enjoy, and you have more discretionary time to pursue a variety of other enjoyable and meaningful activities.

The second and most common way of preparing for retirement is to simply start *saving as much as possible as early as possible*. The idea is to consistently contribute to your retirement fund until you have enough money that you can quit your job and live the rest of your life on that saved money. The retirement fund is normally invested in a diversified portfolio.

Diversification means that you invest in a mix of stocks, bonds, real estate, assets that run counter to the market, and other assets that represent different financial niches. You can further diversify by using mutual funds that put together a mix of stocks, bonds or real estate. The idea is that by diversifying you guard against "having all your eggs in one basket."

For example, if you have in your portfolio of one thousand different stocks five stocks that radically drop in value, your total worth will probably not be affected much. If you had only invested in those five stocks as your total portfolio, you would be in bad financial shape. I advise you to use financial planners to help you guide this approach. They can help you plan for how much you will need when you retire and, of course, recommend how to balance and diversify your savings. However, you do not just turn over your money to someone and ask them to take care of it. You need to be a student of the financial planning process, be an active participant in it, and take ultimate responsibility for any decisions made.

One final note of caution: Beware of the "deprival trap." It goes like this: John and Mary start saving for retirement early in their married life. They save so enthusiastically for their future that they seldom or never have any fun in their present. They don't allow themselves to have some of the joyful experiences that we all need once in a while. They spend forty or fifty years in a constant state of deprival waiting for the day when they retire and can do all the things they always wanted to do. When they finally retire, they are afraid to spend any money because they fear they might outlive their savings. Eventually, they die and their children inherit their savings and spend it on useless consumer stuff.

You don't have to live that scenario. If you consistently save 10 to 20 percent of your income first, invest it, and let the earnings compound starting as early in life as possible, you have your savings covered. Then you can live on and enjoy the eighty to ninety percent of your income you have left. You can enjoy the journey to retirement as much as you think you will enjoy those golden years.

I need to explain the "Rule of 72" as a way to show how savings can grow over time. Simply divide the average reinvested gains you're expecting from your investment into 72 to see about how many years it will take to double your original deposit.

For example, suppose you have an investment of $100,000, anticipate average gains of 10 percent per year, and plan to reinvest all of the gains. To determine how long it will take your original $100,000 to double into $200,000, divide the 10 into 72. The answer is around 7.2 years. If you get the same 10 percent gain over the next seven or so years, your investment will be worth $400,000.

Now what if you need to know how large the yearly rate gain on your investment must be for your original amount to double within a specified time? Divide the number of years you have to achieve the desired amount into 72.

Using the amounts in the previous example, suppose you need to double your original investment of $100,000 in five years. **What yearly rate gain will accomplish that goal if you reinvest all your gains? By dividing 5 into 72, you find that you'll need an annual rate gain of at least 14.4 percent.**

Of course, these are estimates that will be influenced by changes in the markets but they show the power of saving early and consistently. *Note: The Rule of 72 calculates only what happens to an initial sum of money. It does not reflect the huge effect on your savings if you are consistently adding money into it.*

At this point, you might be wondering how your Social Security benefit will sooner or later fit into your retirement plans. My advice is not to factor it into your plans at all. That way, should the government decide to reduce the program or even eliminate it entirely before you retire, you won't be caught unprepared. By planning ahead as though Social Security doesn't exist, you'll never have to make up for a monthly check you were counting on but that didn't materialize. On the other hand, if you *do* wind up collecting Social Security, you'll have an unexpected bonus each month.

The third approach to retirement is what I will call the entrepreneurial or business route. This is where you invest in your own business and grow the business so it becomes your source of retirement income. When it comes time for you to retire, you can sell the business, run it part time, or train someone to run it for you while you do all those things you always wanted to do. You still might invest in a conventional diversified financial portfolio, but you mainly invest what would normally be your savings in growing your own company. This way you can have more direct control over your assets. You are not dependent on the markets or other forces over which you have little or no control. (However, as a company owner, you will find that there will be other forces over which you will not have control.) Depending on your personality and skill set, this might be the way you want to go.

Millionaires are very often average people who get an idea they really believe in, start their own businesses around that idea, work hard, work smart, and are persistent. They are successful because they are devoted to their businesses and enjoy their work. It is a viable approach for many people. However, the downside to this approach must be noted. When you start a business, you are essentially putting all of your eggs in one basket, and you often have to borrow money for your startup. Additionally, the vast majority of new companies fail in their early years. Not an approach for the faint-hearted.

You might also want to consider a hybrid approach that is some combination of the three above. As you move through your life, you might shift from one retirement approach to another. For example, you might be taking the conventional approach but find that you want more direct control over your money. So you cash out some or most of your savings and start a business that you have researched and feel is worth the risk. The choices are yours, but now you have some alternatives to the conventional approach to retirement.

One more thing, if you have done your best trying to save enough money to live a reasonable life in retirement but for whatever reasons haven't saved enough, consider moving to a location where the cost of living is less. That does not just mean a different location only in your state or in your country, but should include anywhere in the world. Even if you don't move, the research will be fun and enlightening.

There is obviously much more to gaining and maintaining your financial security than I have included in this chapter. The ideas are an introduction to some fundamentals of accumulating and utilizing wealth. I hope this has been useful. I hope you have been intrigued enough to want to continue educating yourself about your financial future. For that reason I have listed some key words and phrases below which you can use to further your personal research:

- Price and cost.

- Costs and benefits analysis.

- Increasing income, decreasing costs, or both.

- Responsibility is ultimately yours.

- Live within your means.

- Vocations and avocations.

- Pay your future first.

- 401(k) option matching funds.

- Do what you love to do, maybe.

- Rule of 72.

- Have a crisis or emergency fund.

- Start saving as early as possible.

- Diversification.

- Greed.

- Credit cards and installments.

- Paying interest versus collecting interest.

- Delaying gratification.

- Short-term and long-term thinking.

- Opportunity costs.

- Tradeoffs.

- Investing.

- Guarantees and warranties.

- Cash versus credit.

- Assets versus liabilities.

- Unintended consequences.

- Quality and quantity.
- Get-rich-quick schemes and scams.
- Consistency in saving.
- Psychic income.
- Comparison shopping.
- Enjoying what you have already.
- Is obtaining wealth worth the effort?
- Vested interests.
- Get a variety of input, do research.
- Make informed decisions.
- Financial planning and planners.
- Is anything really "free?"
- What is a good economic transaction?
- Value added.
- Lotteries, gambling.
- Selling techniques used on you.
- Advertising/propaganda.
- Inflation/deflation.
- Entrepreneurship.
- Investing in yourself.
- Wealth through minimalism.

FACTOR 4

Mastering and Using Problem-Solving and Critical-Thinking Skills

Critical-thinking, problem-solving, decision-making, and a host of other practical skills can be used to improve our lives the instant we start using them. These skills are methods of doing our thinking more precisely, efficiently, and effectively. Skills are defined here as methods of doing something. A skill can be described, taught, learned, practiced, and improved. Although skills are often associated with playing sports and other physical activities, they are addressed here as mental activities such as analyzing propaganda, recognizing fallacies of logic, and making decisions. *The number of these mental skills you can acquire and effectively use will greatly influence how successful you will be physically, mentally, financially, socially, and as a steward of our environment.* Although I have taught these strategies, used them in my personal life, and even developed some of them, none were taught to me in my formal education with the exception of a very brief and inadequate explanation of the scientific method.

There are many of these skills—too many to include in this book. I will explain a few of the most basic ones and then give you a listing of important terms, concepts, and ideas that you can pursue in your further research.

The Importance of Words

As a writer and speaker, I love words, but words are easy to misuse and abuse. Take the word "democracy," for example. We in the United States say we are a democracy. We have fought wars in the name of democracy. Millions of U.S. military personnel have died and been casualties of those wars fought largely in the name of democracy. Yet the United States does not have an official definition of democracy. Is it any wonder that we have been so surprised when we "liberate" a country from their dictator so they can be democratic only to find that they can't make their democracy work like we think it should? If we don't have an agreed-upon definition of democracy, how can we know if it is working for us, let alone for others?

I suggest that the following operational definition (a definition that states how the term works) is a good one to use and should be adopted as our national definition. It was developed by one of my mentors, Dr. Ernest Bayles, and reads like this: "Democracy is a process whereby people have an equal opportunity to participate in making group decisions and an equal obligation to abide by those decisions until they are revised or rescinded." Note that democracy *is a process and does not guarantee that good decisions will be made.* People are given the equal opportunity to participate in making the decisions, but they are not required to participate. However, they should understand that not participating is giving up their right to protect their own self-interests. Once the decision is made, everyone is obligated to abide by the decision whether they participated or not and regardless of whether they agree with the decision. However, the definition leaves open the opportunity to change or rescind the decision if it is found to be unworkable. This definition describes a pure democracy, where those who have to abide by the decisions personally participate in the decision-making. Examples could be family meetings, town hall meetings in smaller communities, business meetings, or decision-making in small organizations.

When a group gets very large, and all cannot easily attend decision-making meetings, we resort to "representative democracy," in which all the people who have to abide by the decision have an equal opportunity to elect people from among them to be their representatives in the decision-making bodies. This greatly complicates the system as seen by the state and national governments today. Who do we elect? Can we trust them to act in our best interests? Or will they act in the best interests of those who financially supported them? Will they do post-election what they said they would do pre-election? Are they good decision-makers? Are their values and beliefs consistent with ours? Perhaps someday, with advances in technology, we will again get to directly participate in more pure democratic forums, but today we are largely represented by those we elect. The absence of having a clear definition of a word as important as democracy is unmistakable when we add up the lives and resources that have been used to defend and propagate this key word. As decision-makers, we must be precise in communicating the meanings of words we use.

Other words we use are equally difficult to define, but we go about using them as if we all share the same meanings. Take the word *love*. It has many definitions and nuances, yet many people profess their love for one another and even take vows of marriage without ever discussing exactly what each of them means by the word. Our world is full of these abstract words that we use all the time, and we take for granted that others have the same definitions as we do. Some of those words are "beautiful," "ugly," "conservative," "liberal," "delicious," "good," "bad," "backward," "uncivilized," "better," "worse," "stupid," "intelligent, "handsome," "quality," "nice" and "adequate." These are words that need to be defined as we use them because they are too vague and imprecise to be used to solve problems and make important decisions.

Note that I have put quotation marks around the abstract words to indicate that I know the words are abstract and I want you to know, too. You might want to do the same in your writings. In speech you will often see people using the quotation marks with their hands to indicate they know the word or phrase is abstract. You should ask those who use these abstract words to explain what they mean. Ask them to give you their definitions and clear examples. If you forget to give definitions or examples when you use these words and are asked to do so, you should be glad to do so. The discussion or decision is more likely to be a good one if it is based on mutual understandings of the words being used.

Here are some additional suggestions for better communication taken from the study of semantics:

- **Use concrete words that can be detected by your senses as much as possible.** That is, words that describe something you can see, smell, touch, hear, or taste. Otherwise, you are using the abstract words which are only thoughts and are harder to define and explain.

- **Be careful using "is" and "are," because our minds can easily interpret them to mean one hundred percent or equal.** For example, if you say that "Jim is stupid," the hearer can easily interpret that to mean that "Jim is one hundred percent stupid" or that "Jim equals stupid." You probably meant to say that some aspect or aspects of Jim's behavior was inappropriate, not that he is completely stupid in every way. Also, what did you mean by "stupid?"

- **All analogies are eventually false, so if you use an analogy you should feel obligated to point that out.** For example, a person who had never seen an airplane before would probably describe it by comparing it to a bird. When I lived in Tanzania in the late 1960s, the word for airplane in Swahili, "ndege," was also the word for bird. So be careful when you use analogies and point out the dissimilarities as well as the similarities.

- **Be wary of using all-inclusive words such as "all," "always," "every," "never" and "entirely."** These words are saying that whatever you are describing is one hundred percent that way. For example, you might describe your Uncle Joe as "never on time." But unless you follow your uncle around one hundred percent of the time, you cannot make that statement. Maybe he has been late to all of the meetings he has had with you. Surely he is on time once in a while, such as when he meets his buddies at the local bar. Your uncle is actually "often late" or "usually late."

- **Words only represent things and ideas, but they are not the things or the ideas.** Sometimes words can cause such strong emotions in people that they act on the words themselves. For example, when I was a youth, the word "communist" was feared and hated so much by some Americans that to be called a communist or be associated with communism in any way could get people in deep trouble. Many of those who were so against the word "communism" probably could not define how communism works, but they were sure it and anyone associated with it was "bad."

- **Even more basic to communication is that when you say a word to me, you cannot assume that I have the same interpretation of that word that you do.** It is quite possible that if you say "X," I might interpret it as "Y." It is similar to interpreting from one language to another except that it is interpreting from one mind to another mind, but in the same language. If you have any doubt about a listener's understanding you, a good strategy is to ask him or her to repeat your idea or give an original example.

- **Be cautious of people (and yourself) using words that set up "either-or" and "good-bad" situations.** These dichotomies are most often not indicative of reality. For example, country A declares war on country B. The leader of country A tells the leader of country C that "You are either for us going to war or you are against us. If you are for us going to war, you are our friend; and if you are against us going to war, you are our enemy." The leader of country C is forced into an either-or choice when he or she may be partly in agreement and partly not in agreement with starting the war. There is no room to negotiate or explain a nuance when you are forced into a black-and-white situation. Also, most situations in the real world are not black-and-white but are varying shades of gray.

- **Be suspicious of people who claim personal authority.** These would be people who expect you to believe anything they tell you because they have some special power they can't explain to you. Or they have a special relationship with the supernatural that only they have and they can't teach it to you. Or they have a secret way to interpret the truth from old writings, manuscripts, crystal balls, or the lines in your hands that you should just accept without question—and maybe even pay them for.

- **Keep in mind that change is probably the most constant thing in the universe.** We change, the environment changes, others change, and our ideas change. That is why it is wise to think of your ideas and beliefs as being dated. For example, someone might have supported segregation in the 1950s and '60s but then worked for integration for the rest of her life after having had some close relationships and friendships with those she formerly disliked and mistrusted. As an aside, note that it is *not* fair for one politician to accuse another of a "flip-flop" just because he or she changed positions on an issue. It is fair to ask why the politician changed positions. The answer should include wording such as, "I changed because of these reasons (then list the reasons). I am a different person with some different ideas than I had previously. I don't just make up my mind and close it to new information. I base my ideas and beliefs on the newest and most reliable information possible. If new ideas cause me to change or modify my beliefs, then I will change them." Of course, if the politician cannot give valid reasons for the change … Gotcha.

In closing this section I want to again emphasize the need to use qualifying words and phrases, and to avoid using absolutes, especially when stating conclusions, theories, or findings. Use phraseology such as "At this point …" or "As best we can tell with this data …" or "A strong case can be made for …" or "The research I recently completed suggests that …"

All History Is Interpretation

There are a lot of sayings about the importance of understanding history so we don't make the same mistakes again, and it's said that understanding history will enable us to better understand today. I have taken many history classes and read many history books. I have even written some history and helped a friend write his history book. It hasn't been until recently that I realized that in all this time *I have never read or heard anyone say what to me seems very obvious; that all history is in varying degrees interpretation.* The writer of history reads and interprets histories written and interpreted by others. A thoroughly documented history book will contain hundreds of documents that are based on hundreds of other documents, all of which have been interpreted at the time of their writing and at the time of their reading. All the writers and readers bring their individual unique views, beliefs, experiences, and biases to the written page. The results are all sorts of interpretations of a given event or period in the past.

But what about now with our technologies of all sorts? Isn't the television newscast video recording of an event exactly what happened?

Photography as history is not much different than the written word in that it is still interpretive. Even though a picture is usually clearer and more representative of what happened than a written description, it is still full of interpretations. For example, a news agency cameraman is covering a story where protesters are being engaged by police. This is history in the making. The cameraman has the choice of shooting his footage in any direction of a 360-degree circle. Which direction does he choose to shoot? If he points his camera south, he misses what is happening in the other three directions. If he pans his camera in the total 360 degrees, the most important event might be happening in the east when he is pointing his camera west. Also, after he has taken several minutes or even hours of footage, he or his editors will choose only a few minutes or seconds of the total raw film to be shown on the news that night. The viewers of the program will then see the news item, and they interpret this recent history from their personal vantage points. The person who values law and order will probably see something different than the person who places high value on the right to demonstrate.

101

The point here is that if we are going to use history to try to understand the past, we need to keep in mind that we are not discovering what actually happened in the past. We are discovering what the recorders of the past interpreted as being the record of the past. I remember a history textbook I had in school that was titled *The History of the United States*. I thought it was the *total* history of our country. The title should have been *A History of the United States*. An introduction to the book should have emphasized that this was the best version of our country's history that the writer or writers could compile given restrictions such as time, resources, ability, and the publisher's guidelines. It should have included at least a short paragraph stating that no one can write a complete history of the United States. It is just not possible to include everything because we don't know everything.

It also should be pointed out that other variables are involved in producing the historical record. The first is the writer's ability as a writer. Poor prose writers of history do not often become popular historians. The second is that writers want to choose topics or personalities that will be interesting to readers. Writers and their publishers want and need to sell books. The need to sell books might trump the need to write the most accurate account of a period of history. A good example of this was when a publisher of American history textbooks for public schools had different versions of the same text for the northern and southern sections of the country. The differences were mainly in the ways that the Civil War and Reconstruction periods were presented. History was *adjusted* to meet market demand.

Even though recording history is constantly being refined, it can never be totally objective. Developing a historical record has to involve a lot of interpretation, as does the reading or watching of it. I encourage you to approach historical references with a healthy degree of skepticism.

Three Ways of Observing and Reporting Data

Whether we are using a formal method of problem-solving or are going about our everyday activities, we are constantly observing what goes on around us. We process what we see to ourselves by our thinking and then to others by communicating with them through our words. In either case we want to be as precise as possible when we report what we observe. For example, pretend you are a customer in a restaurant. You observe a waitress deliver a plate of food to another customer. Before the waitress can leave the table, the male customer begins yelling at the waitress. The waitress turns away and goes back to the kitchen. There are three ways you could report your observation.

1. You might **describe your observation.** Using the situation above, you would say something like the following: "A female dressed as a waitress brought a plate of food to a male customer and immediately was yelled at by the customer. I couldn't hear what was said. The waitress turned away from the table and went into the kitchen." When you objectively describe what you saw to the best of your ability, you are giving a simple description. You are acting like a camera as best you can. If you are a witness in a court of law, the judge only wants to hear facts from you. Getting factual descriptions is very important in decision-making in courts of justice. It is also important to get factual observations because they constitute the data of experiments. When enough people report the same description of the same event, we are able to call the sum of those observations a fact. Reliable facts are the basis of the scientific method and of all effective decision-making.

2. You might **make an inference** about your observation. Using the same situation above you might say something like, "The customer was really upset by the poor service he was getting and took out his anger on the waitress." Because you did not hear what was said, you made an inference (guess) about what caused the yelling by the customer. If you put this in scientific terms, it would be a hypothesis. It is something that would have to be tested to see if you guessed correctly. In this instance you made an inference or guess and then stated it as if it were a fact. If you asked someone nearer to the table you observed, he might tell you that the man was angry because the waitress was his girlfriend and he saw her out with another man

last night. Your inference was wrong. Your reporting was incorrect. You guessed outside the facts.

3. You might **make a value judgment** about what you observed. In this case you might say something like, "This restaurant has really low-life clients. I won't come here again." In this case you would have made an even worse report of your observation. Based on one incident, you jumped to a conclusion that the clients of the restaurant were so unsavory that you will never come here again. You do not have enough evidence to make such a judgment about the restaurant. The food might be wonderful, and this might be the first incident or disruption to ever happen. These kinds of judgments are even greater stumbling blocks to good decision-making than making inferences. You went beyond the incident you observed and made a judgment about the quality of all the clients of the restaurant.

I hope this explanation has shown the importance of objective observations and how even more important it is that they are reported and used at the objective level. Remember, report like a camera as best you can.

Basic Decision-Making Steps

At the time I am writing this book many of those who are representing us at the state and national levels of government are behaving as if they know nothing about decision-making. For example, some of the representatives and their constituents actually view "compromise" as a dirty word and view those who are willing to use compromise as being "weak." I would like to explain to these folks and anyone else who will listen about how the decision-making process can work and why the steps are important.

Let me use an example from my childhood to illustrate the steps. I lived in a semirural area outside Kansas City. We kids did not have ball fields and organized sports. We would show up at someone's house with whatever balls and equipment we had. It often resulted in a situation like the following:

Several of us met at Jerry's house because his backyard was the biggest, wasn't on much of a hill, and didn't have as many trees to get in the way of our games. It often happened that we would have several kids show up usually with some baseball equipment and others with some football equipment. We had to decide which we were going to play. If everyone agreed to play one sport, there was no problem. Everyone got what he or she wanted. We had consensus, and everyone was happy to abide by our decision.

If we had some kids who wanted to play football and some who wanted to play baseball, we tried to get a compromise so each group got part of what they wanted but realizing nobody got everything they wanted. We might agree that we would play football for one hour and then play baseball for one hour. Nobody was completely happy, but since we all got part of what we wanted, we were happy enough to voluntarily go along with the decision.

If we could not get a compromise we would usually vote, and the game that got the most votes is what we played the total time. This, of course, meant that those who won the vote were happy and those who lost the vote were not happy. Some got all they wanted and others got nothing they wanted. The "losers" usually did not enjoy themselves as much as the winners and often went home earlier than the rest.

On the few occasions when some of the kids refused to consider anything but playing their game the total time, we usually broke up and went home with no one getting to play anything. In a way, everybody was a loser.

One other option we did *not* use. We could have had a physical fight (a mini war) and the winners could have forced the losers to play the winners' game. As kids, we knew that wouldn't work ... unlike many national "leaders" today.

A major point I want to make is that decision-makers can evolve the process. Start with attempting to get consensus, then try compromise, then majority vote—and avoid violence. The key to this is that as the process evolves from consensus onward, the degree of voluntary compliance to the decision decreases. The less the voluntary compliance the more the decision will need to be policed. Too many of those in decision-making positions do not seem to understand the voluntary compliance part of the process. The use of compromise is a legitimate and useful strategy when making group decisions and has a reasonable chance of getting voluntary compliance. The only weakness of compromising is the weak thinking of those who refuse to even consider it as a strategy.

The Best Approach to Solving Problems Is Preventing Them

A major reason for writing this book is to make available useful knowledge that can be applied to our lives. If we base our lifestyles on the best knowledge available, we can prevent or at least lessen the problems in our lives. It is hugely disappointing to read study after study that indicates major causes of disease and death in the United States are preventable simply by changing our lifestyle habits. By eating real, unprocessed, plant-based food as the major part of our nutritional intake; getting reasonable exercise; not smoking; drinking mostly water for our liquids; and being lifelong students of physical health, we could substantially improve our personal and national health. We would lessen the strain on our medical system. We would save money personally and as a nation.

We wouldn't have to rely on as many medicines, doctor visits, operations, and transplants. Yet most of the money for medical research is spent on finding *cures* for the diseases, not on the *prevention* of the diseases.

Those of us who practice and promote healthy lifestyles are overwhelmed and drowned out by the multinational industries who use huge budgets to advertise manufactured and processed foods that are not healthy. Even worse, they aim much of that marketing at children. Teach the children early to develop tastes for fats, sugars, and salt. Industry knows that it is important to get the kids hooked early because it is difficult for most people to break bad habits. You and I must be promoters of programs and practices in preschools and all through our school systems that stress teaching, modeling, and developing lifestyles that prevent problems of all types.

As discussed above, it is very clear what we need to do to live physically healthier lives. The chapter on mental health gives ideas such as positive thinking, controlling your thinking, and reducing stress, which can minimize mental health problems. The chapter on financial planning gives ideas such as early savings plans, reducing spending, distinguishing between wants and desires, and considering alternative ways of retiring. All of these will reduce financial problems if they are implemented. The chapter on responsibility discusses ways in which we can prevent or lessen social and environmental problems. It also is a final reminder to you that you need to take ultimate responsibility for yourself because we need you to be highly functioning if we are going to be successful in this revolution.

My final point about prevention is that in order to prevent something from happening, we need to know how it works. If I know how my car works, I will know why I should change the oil at the appropriate intervals. I know that if I spend a few dollars on an oil change, I can save thousands by preventing the need for a new engine. If I know how the sewage system works, I know to prevent the dumping of used oil, old insecticides, and out-of-date medicine down the drain or toilet. To do so is not being responsible to myself, others, or the environment. I can prevent myself from financial insecurity if I know how compound interest works. I will know why I should save as much as possible, as early as possible and as consistently as possible to gain financial security. Finding out how things work is fascinating and can give us insight into what we can do to prevent problems so we don't have to go to the trouble and expense of solving them. That sounds like a really good case for lifelong learning.

Knowing the Difference between Form and Substance

One of the major problems I have found in problem-solving is the inability of people to distinguish between form and substance. Form refers to how something looks if it is an object or how something is done if it applies to activities of some type. The form of my car (an object or thing) is how it is shaped, its lines, its beauty, or lack thereof. The form of education (an activity) is the teaching and learning processes or methods teachers use.

Substance refers to the fundamental quality of something, the usefulness of it, the basic purpose or the practical importance.

The substance of my car, therefore, is to transport me from place to place. I want it to be safe, economical, and reliable. That is its practical importance. The substance of education is the content of what I learn or should learn. A substantive education teaches me knowledge and skills that I can use to be self-reliant, healthy, and responsible.

I can remember a time when American automobile companies were concentrating on the form of their cars and seemed to disregard the substance of them. The cars grew bigger and longer for no apparent reasons. Odd-shaped fenders (tail fins) and two- and three-tone paint jobs were common, and various tail lights were added for their supposedly attractive shapes. At that time you expected for your American car to start having problems around 50,000 miles. The cars were difficult to handle and had no safety features. The accent was on form, and little attention was made to substance. When Japanese cars started to be imported into the United States, the American public found them to be reliable, easy to drive, economical to own, and less expensive to purchase. They were not as attractive (form) but they had the transportation features (substance) that made them desirable.

In the last few decades American automobile manufacturers have been forced to be more competitive by concentrating their efforts on the substance of their cars. Because of wind-tunnel experiments to achieve better gas mileage, autos today have pretty much the same aerodynamic shape. Now everyone seems to be emphasizing substance—quality—with form a lesser concern.

American education is an example of how the emphasis on form has never been overcome. The substance of education remains substantially unchanged. Even though much in the world has changed greatly, our education system still teaches pretty much the same things as it has for many decades.

There have been and are now attempts to change education in positive ways, and none of them have worked or will work.

The reason is that the changes have all been attempts to change form. Some examples are lengthening the school day or calendar year, building open classrooms, reorganizing how classes are configured, team teaching, reducing the size of classes, getting parents more involved, reducing administration, funding schools more, combining districts, paying teachers more, having charter schools, using vouchers, having higher standards, having traditional schools, and so on.

There have been even more attempts to change schools for the better, and all these attempts have two things in common. One, they have all failed to improve education. And two, none of them substantially change the substance of education—what is being taught and maybe learned. There have been no real analyses or challenges to the present curriculum. For all practical purposes the courses in schools today are the same courses I took in the 1950s. Some courses have been added, such as those in math, but they are just more of the same. There has been no systematic analysis of what is needed for education to survive and thrive in the twenty-first century.

This book is the result of my personal analysis of what needs to be the "new basics" of education in our schools. These new basics would involve classes, experiences, modeling, and living the five factors as a starting point. When we as a nation are becoming increasingly obese and sickly, don't we need to teach and model the gaining and maintaining of physical health? As drug use and mental illnesses increase, shouldn't we be teaching how to gain and maintain mental health? As individual debt increases, job markets change, and people live longer but not necessarily healthier, shouldn't we be educating youth about how to gain and maintain financial security? As we become increasingly aware of humans' impact on our environment, shouldn't we be addressing our responsibilities to the earth as a whole and to the communities in which we live? Given that we have developed technology much faster than we have developed our human relations, isn't it wise to at least ponder what our responsibilities are to our fellow man? Given that we have only a few decades to live the miracles of lives we have been given, doesn't it make sense for us to think about what our responsibilities are to make these lives as meaningful as possible?

I will keep working to improve and promote the five factors and hope you will find it worth your time to take some part in attempting this revolution.

Using the Scientific Method

The scientific method is simply a general process used to solve problems and explain how things work. It is one of the greatest discoveries of all time, yet it is simple to understand and apply. You and I are acting like scientists all the time even if we don't know it. For example, pretend you are happily making a vegetable stew like the one you had at your mother's house and can't remember what spices were in it. You want to call your mother but can't find your cell phone. You have a problem. You need to *gather some facts,* so you try to remember the last time you had the phone. Was it in the car, in the living room, or in your purse in the closet? Your best guess (hypothesis) is that your phone is in the living room. You test your hypothesis by going into the living room and looking around. You are using the scientific "If, then" statement, but you probably don't actually state it. The statement would be "If I am going to find my phone, then I will find it in the living room."

In the living room you look on the tables, under the couch and under cushions of the couch and chairs, yet you cannot find the phone. You have disproved your hypothesis and must develop another hypothesis: If I look in the car, then I will find my phone. You go to the car and don't find it. Then you guess it is in your purse in the closet and you look there. Still no phone. You have run out of your original hypotheses but come up with another. You ask your daughter if she has seen your phone. You discover that she used it when her phone battery was not charged and it is in her room. The problem is solved. This is a very simple problem that has a clear solution, but it should illustrate the basic format of the scientific method. We discover a problem, then gather information we hope will help us get a solution, then use the information to formulate a hypothesis or guess to the solution, and then test the hypothesis to see if our guess is a good one.

Most problems are far more complex and have more variables that are difficult to control. For an example, let me explain how I arrived at the conclusion and solution (tentative) about nutrition in the chapter on physical health.

Let me state now that I have found the main thing people do not understand about the scientific method is that scientists do not consider the answers to most problems to be absolute or final. A diligent scientist always cautions that his or her solution today might be changed tomorrow based on new information. Science is always adjusting and reformulating findings based on new data and discoveries. This drives some people crazy because they want answers that will always be true regardless of changes in the world or the introduction of new data. A good scientist will tell you something like the following: "This is the best solution I can determine at this time based on the facts I have and under the present circumstances. Please keep an open mind to new data that might logically lead to an adjustment of the present conclusion."

Now let's go back to how I used the scientific method to determine what to write about nutrition in the chapter on physical health. My problem was to determine what nutritional lifestyle I should recommend. Remember this is just one of the answers I have been *seeking for decades* based on my question "What's worth knowing?" I have been constantly doing research (which I find is more fun than nearly all forms of the usual human forms of "entertainment") about the factors in this book. My questions, hypotheses, experiments, and conclusions have evolved and changed many dozens and even hundreds of times for some topics. Older conclusions are replaced by newer conclusions based on new findings as I become aware of them. I also apply what I have learned in graduate classes about experimental design and statistics to check the appropriateness of the research. My ultimate experiment is to personally practice each new finding for myself to see if it works for me. If it doesn't work for me, then I don't suggest it to others.

My nutritional research and my personal diet lifestyle evolved over the decades to what you have already read earlier in the book. To make it easy to remember and to allow for research yet to be done, I summarized those findings down to basically eating a wide variety of plant-based, natural food. As a sidelight, at one time I considered the chapter finished and had saved it in final form but then read a book by Dr. Joel Fuhrman called *Eat to Live*. His research was generally consistent with my research, but his findings on nutritional values of various foods were new and important insights that caused me to add to my chapter that green leafy vegetables should be a featured part of the plant-based diet. I did this only after I made that change in my own diet and experienced desirable results. Even though I was already eating a wide variety of plant-based foods, the addition of more green leafy vegetables caused my skin to become clearer, made me feel more satisfied after meals, and caused my weight to stabilize in the middle of the desirable range. I have no doubt that I will find other changes I will want to make based on new evidence after the book is published. That is good and to be expected, because the continual application of the scientific method should lead to improvements with each change.

As you do your own research about nutrition, keep on the lookout for two different kinds of scientists or people posing as scientists. I think you will find that the true scientist will be trying to help you attain a healthier state of being. The "scientist" who has "sold out" or the person who is posing as a scientist will be trying to sell you a commercial product to make you thinner, more attractive, or in some way more desirable but not necessarily healthier.

Human Consequences of Decision-Making Matrix

There was a time in my career in education when there was a new but poorly developed fad to teach problem-solving. It did not consist of strategies and skills such as those in this book. It pretty much consisted of a teacher dividing the class into several groups and giving them a problem to solve. The problems could be small ones that could be solved in a day or two, or large ones that could require several days to allow students to do extended research. At some point each of the groups would report their findings and how they determined their solution to the rest of the class. After all the groups had reported their results, there would be a justifiable concern about the quality of the solutions to the problems. Which solution was best? Since there were no standards to judge the value of the decisions, the teacher would then say something like, "You all did a good job, and this shows how different people can solve the same problem in different ways. We all have our opinions and are entitled to our opinions." Although the students might have learned some research, planning, and communication skills, they also learned that one solution is just as good as another. This is not a good theory on which to run your life, your family or your nation's government. If you have several solutions to a problem, you need a way to judge those solutions to decide which one should be implemented. Here is the strategy I devised to solve this problem.

I suggest that we judge the value of decisions on the consequences they will have to human beings and the environment. We should try our best to determine both the positive and the negative consequences of our decision if we act on it. Here are the questions we should ask ourselves as we determine whether or not we should implement a decision:

- What are the positive and the negative *consequences to me* in the short term and the long term?

- What are the positive and the negative consequences to others in the short term and the long term?

- What are the positive and the negative consequences to the environment in the short term and the long term?

Most people who have used this method prefer to use it in the form of a matrix. The matrix is useful for individual decision-making or in a group setting.

HUMAN CONSEQUENCES

DECISION-MAKING MATRIX

	SHORT-TERM CONSEQUENCES		LONG-TERM CONSEQUENCES	
	POSITIVE	NEGATIVE	POSITIVE	NEGATIVE
CONSEQUENSES TO SELF				
CONSEQUENSES TO OTHERS	POSITIVE / NEGATIVE		POSITIVE / NEGATIVE	
CONSEQUENSES TO THE ENVIRONMENT	POSITIVE / NEGATIVE		POSITIVE / NEGATIVE	

Obviously, you want to be aware of what will happen to you as an individual if the decision is implemented. It is easiest to determine what will happen to you in the short term. Note that being concerned only about the consequences to you in the short term and ignoring the other cells is called "immature behavior." It is much more difficult to determine what your consequences will be in the long term. When you try to determine the long-term consequences, you are trying to seek out those elusive unintended consequences that we have all experienced when we acted immaturely. You will have to determine how you will define "short term" and "long term." They will probably be determined in large part by the type of decision you are making. You may find it best to express terms in a range, such as a short-term range of zero to five years and a long-term range of six to twenty years.

You will find it more difficult to predict who else besides yourself will be impacted by your decision, especially in the long term. If appropriate, you might want to seek the input of people you think will be affected. They could tell you what they think might happen and if they saw the consequences to them as positive or negative. You also might ask a third party or parties who are *not involved* in the decision to help for their objective input.

You might not use consequences to the environment as much when you are making very personal decisions—although decisions such as purchasing a house, choosing means of transportation, planning landscaping, and deciding on forms of leisure activities have some environmental implications. Environmental consequences will be more evident when making larger decisions at neighborhood, city, state, and more far-reaching levels. Determining environmental consequences at these levels will demand more formal research.

You may find out very quickly that your decision should not be implemented. For example, you determine that a new job in a different location is opposed by every member of your family—and when you find that the cost of living there is more expensive, you oppose it, too. Or you might find very quickly that you should act on the decision because nearly everything is positive. For example, when I discovered a job opportunity in Africa, my family was immediately very receptive to the experience and ready to sell everything and move to Tanzania for two years. We went and had a fantastic experience while giving service to a third-world country.

It is also possible that you will find that you will need to do such extensive research on the consequences of your decision that you either postpone making the decision or disregard it.

Many users of the matrix have found it useful to give differing weights to some of the variables. For example, consequences to your spouse might be assigned a weight of 3, income a 2, and living conditions a 2.5.

The use of this matrix will not guarantee that good decisions will be made. However, the conscientious use of the matrix to consider the consequences of decisions as measured by what will probably happen to yourself, others, and the environment should decrease the probability that gross harm will occur. In the chapter about your responsibilities to others, the environment and yourself, it will be even clearer how this matrix fits with those variables.

I would love to see this matrix used by individuals, families, businesses, governments, and any other organizations where decisions have to be made. I would like to see the news media use the matrix when they interview politicians. When heads of state meet, I would like them to use the matrix as part of the format of their talks. I would like the matrix to become so familiar and such a habit that it would be automatically the default for most decision-making.

Some Final Thoughts about Decision-Making Tradeoffs

I have found that not understanding the economic concept of tradeoffs can be problematic to some decision-makers. The concept simply means that when you make any decision or choice, you need to be aware that you are automatically giving up all the other possible choices. If you choose to purchase the white car, you are giving up all the other colors of that car. You get something, but you are also giving up something. You decide this, you give up that. If you choose this, you trade off that.

Not being aware of or not accepting the idea of tradeoffs can cause problems for the person who believes a decision should be perfect. This person often has great trouble making a decision because she can never find a perfect one. Making the decision becomes a long and dragged-out affair that wears her out. Maybe she never makes a decision on the matter even though it is an important one. If she accepts the reality that there are always tradeoffs, she can proceed and make the best choice possible and enjoy the fruits of her decision.

The other problem I see is when someone makes a decision and immediately starts second-guessing himself. He chooses the white car and on the way out of the dealership he starts thinking that the black car looks richer than his white one, or the red car seems sportier. If he understood tradeoffs, maybe he would be more careful in making his decision, forget what he rejected, and thoroughly enjoy his well-chosen white Zipmobile XLZ.

Sunk Costs

The concept of *sunk costs* also comes from the study of economics, and it also has important implications in many aspects of life. *Sunk costs* refers to time, energy, and other resources that have been used up and are gone. We can't get them back. For example, pretend I was the originator and owner of the Square Tire Manufacturing Corporation and had been in business for five years. I had never made a profit no matter what I did. I put the best materials into my tires. I had a great marketing plan, hired top-notch workers and gave ten-year warranties on my tires. One day my accountant matter-of-factly tells me that I need to close down our plant and liquidate everything. I reply that I could never do that. I explain that I have invested more than five years of my life and spent millions of dollars on this business. I can't quit now. My accountant then patiently explains that if I continue to operate the business, I will also continue to use up my life and my fortune. He explains further that I should count those years and those dollars as sunk costs. They are gone. I cannot get them back and I need to forget about them. My decision about my business should not be made looking back at my investments but should be made looking forward to the future.

A sad but very relevant example of *sunk costs* not being recognized was when I was a new teacher in a middle school in Kansas. I was in our teachers' lounge and overheard an older math teacher telling a colleague that he hated being a teacher. He hated the students and they hated him. Every day was a battle with the enemy, his students. The thing I remember most was when he said, "I only have nine more years to retirement. I can't wait to get out of here."

When I asked him why he didn't quit this job that he hated so much, he told me that he couldn't because he had worked hard to get his degree and certification to teach and he couldn't give that up. He was going to go through nine more years of self-described hell based on a four-year investment that he knew was a bad one years ago. If he had understood *sunk costs*, he would have at least considered finding new work that he could enjoy for the rest of his life and forget about the time, effort, and money that he had expended so long ago, that he could not retrieve, and that is now irrelevant to his decision about his future.

This example was so strong and clear that I have described it in many situations. As a dean of a college of education, I traditionally gave a final address to each class of our graduating teachers. In every one of those speeches I cautioned the new teachers that someday they might find out that they are not happy or fulfilled as a teacher. If they find that to be true even after they get help from colleagues and the administration, they should look for employment elsewhere. They would be doing themselves, their students and their profession a favor.

Our decisions need to be made on what will make us happy, productive, and fulfilled in the future, not on what we did in that part of our lives that we have already lived.

Make Lists and Prioritize

I was planning a project with a local businessperson. We were listing revisions he was going to make in previous work he had done for me. As we discussed the items, I wrote each one down and noticed that he was not making any notes. I asked him if he needed something to write on to make a list if he wasn't going to put his list on his phone. He assured me that he would remember all the changes. Well, he didn't remember and didn't complete all the tasks we discussed. When the same thing happened again, I replaced him. I wish I could say this is the only time this has happened to me, but it is common enough for me to comment here.

The making of lists to ensure we remember something is so simple and basic, I can't believe I need to mention it. However, while I am on the subject, let me discuss another use of lists beyond that of just remembering what to needs to be done. Many people, especially successful ones, make lists of what they need and want to do during a given day. Once the list is made, they take the time to prioritize the items from the most important to the least important. They start their days working on and completing the most important thing on the list first and then going to the second most important project. This insures that the most important things on the list get completed even if all the items can't be completed in that day.

I have been told by some people that they do not use lists because they do not want the pressure of doing everything in one day. It puts them under too much stress. *They don't realize that using this priority approach takes off the stress because if you don't complete everything, the things not completed were the least important.* Most of the least important things we think we should do can be postponed until the next day or maybe longer without any damage being done. If low-priority items never rise higher in the priority list over time, they might be candidates to be completely dropped from the list.

I have found it to be true that making and prioritizing the list is best done the day before the work is to be done. It can be done as one of the last tasks of the working day or sometime prior to going to bed. This enables your subconscious to work on how to do the tasks as you sleep and you can complete them more efficiently the next day. I can't prove the subconscious theory but I do know it works for me. If you are not currently using prioritized lists as a means to increase your decision-making efficiency, I suggest you try it as a personal experiment for a week or two.

Concentrate on Things You Can Influence

We have never in history had so many ways of getting information. We know about a plane crash in the Arctic moments after it happens. We know if drought and famine are occurring somewhere in Africa. We know if there is a civil war breaking out in a small East European country. We know about increasing signs of ominous environmental changes all over the world.

Not many years ago we obtained news that was much more local and national. Life was simpler then, because we simply didn't know about the world that surrounded us. Now it is very easy for us to focus on what is beyond us and beyond our control rather than focus on what is near us and within us, which is more within our control.

I can do little to control the famines that frequently get reported around the world, but I can do something about making my and my family's diet more nutritious.

I can't control how much it rains to ensure our water supply, but I can do all I can to conserve the water we do have.

I can't control what other people think of me, but I can think about other people and myself in positive and optimistic terms.

I can't change how other people have treated me in the past, but I can treat other people as I would like to be treated or as I think they would like to be treated.

I can't influence much about the international economy, but I can make sure that both the quantity and the quality of my work are something of which I am proud.

I can't control other people's habits, but I can control my own habits so they are compatible with the welfare of others, the environment, and myself.

I can't control what others think is beautiful, but I can personally find the beauty in the things, people, and events that are close to me every day.

You get the idea. Most of the things in this world are beyond your control and my control. But the closer we get to home, the greater our influence and control become. We can't control that dictator in South America, but we can control our diets, exercise, spending and saving, ways of behaving toward others and the environment, and how we think about ourselves. A crucial decision that we can make and practice is to concentrate our efforts on things we can control. It is pretty much covered in an old adage that has been attributed to so many different people, "Change that which can be changed, accept that which cannot be changed, and be wise enough to know the difference between the two."

The following words and terms are listed as guides to your further research in the area of problem-solving and critical thinking:

- Scientific method.

- Semantics.

- Basic statistics.

- Fallacies of logic.

- Propaganda analysis.

- Experimentation.

- Unintended consequences.

- Advertising.

- Sales techniques.

- Question your strongest beliefs.

- Asking correct questions.

- Ask WHY questions before HOW questions.

- Means and ends.

- Form and substance.

- How to conduct a meeting.

- Cause and effect versus correlations.

- Inductive and deductive reasoning.

- Authority or faith versus science.

- Decision-making matrix.

- Concrete versus abstract words.

- Evolution/revolution continuum.

- Discrimination.

- Overgeneralizations.

- Beliefs -> decisions -> actions -> consequences.

- Perspective.

- Paradigms.

- Mindsets.

- Personal research.

- Contingency planning.

- Facts versus opinions.

- Interpretation versus facts.

- Operational definitions.

- Prioritizing.

- Tradeoffs.

- Opportunity costs.

- Sunk costs.

- An answer or the answer.

- Win-win negotiations.

- Change as a constant.

- Open mind to new alternatives.

- Relativity versus absolutism or authoritarianism.

- Creativity.

- Making and using lists.

- Vested interests.

- Specificity (Do sweat the small stuff).

- Performance versus status or education.

- "Sleep on it."

- Inquisitiveness (like a child).

FACTOR 5

Acting Responsibly to Others, the Environment, and Yourself

We live with other people in our families, towns, cities, states, and countries, all over our planet Earth. We human beings come in all sorts of shapes, sizes, skin tones, beliefs, and ways of going about living our lives. However, as we gain more knowledge, we are realizing that we human beings have vastly more in common with each other than we have differences. What ideas, beliefs, and practices have we retained that cause us to distrust, dislike, and sometimes wage war with other humans who are essentially just like us? Do we have any ethical or moral responsibilities to other people?

Planet Earth is a finite place with finite resources. It can provide us with what we need to exist and those things we desire beyond basic living. Some of us have been fortunate enough to be born at a time and in a place where we enjoy the luxuries of great abundance. We have been accused of exploiting that abundance to the detriment of our environment and to the detriment of ourselves and future generations. Do we continue short-sighted practices that devastate our immediate environments and our planet as a whole? Or do we act more responsibly and treat our planet as if we owned it? Because we do.

Each one of us is a miracle. You are a unique individual among all the billions of people in the world. You have the opportunity to live as the most "advanced" creature on Earth. You are in that group that sits on the very top of the food chain. You have this chance to live at a time and in a place that affords you more choices and opportunities than all others have had at any time in history. What are you going to do with this unprecedented opportunity? Do you have any responsibilities to yourself to make the best of this once-in-the-history-of-man opportunity?

Using Basic Ethics as a Basis for Explaining Responsibilities

I am using the term "basic ethics" to mean a simple set of moral principles that people can understand and use to guide their choices throughout their lives. I am choosing these three principles because they are generally agreed upon or implied in most of the sources I have consulted and should be generally accepted. They seem to form a solid basis of ethical thought and practice. They are:

- Do no harm.

- Make things better.

- Be fair.

"Do no harm" is a shortened form of "First, do no harm," which is an oath that many doctors take when they graduate. For the record, it is *not* part of the Hippocratic Oath. I am suggesting that "do no harm" is a basic guideline for living our lives. I will try not to do damage, cause hurt, cause injury, or inflict pain of any kind. In other words, *I will not do deliberate harm to others, my environment, or myself.* I realize there might be situations where I will have to do some harm (as I will discuss in each following section), but I will minimize that harm or hurt as much as possible. I will try to do the least harm possible. There are some unique situations where I might be forced to harm someone in order to prevent him or her from doing a greater harm. However, the doing-no-harm principle seems to be a solid ethical premise.

For example, this principle is the reason I chose to go into the medical corps rather than a combat unit when I was in military service. What do you think the world would look like if everyone was taught early in life to "do no harm," and everyone practiced it? I'll bet the world would look a lot different than it does today.

"Make things better" is another obvious choice of a principle to live by. Just about everything can get better in some way—and why wouldn't you want to make improvements if you could? Later, I will show how this guideline for living can be applied to our acting responsibly toward others, our environment, and ourselves. I can remember when Japanese industries began applying this principle to their manufacturing processes. They increased the quality of their products by making things better everywhere they could. Uniquely for that time, they asked the workers on the assembly lines as well as their supervisors to make suggestions for improving the quality of the product or improving the process of making the product. I am writing this book for the purpose of "making things better." What do you think the world would look like if everyone was taught early in life to "make things better," and everyone practiced it?

"Be fair" means that we seek justice, act honestly, deal fairly, promote equal opportunity and equal treatment, objectively analyze and settle disputes, ensure that people receive what they deserve, and get that to which they are entitled. Being fair is exemplified by the struggle to free slaves in the United States and finally have laws that give them and their descendants equal opportunity to pursue their goals and dreams. Although making those laws operational and a national habit has taken an unforgivable length of time, fairness establishes that everyone has or should have an equal opportunity to be successful. It is just like having a race in a track and field event. Everyone starts from the same starting line and runs the same distance to the finish line. We don't let the kids with light skin have their starting line ten yards closer to the finish line. In the same way a fair business transaction is when there is an exchange of goods, services, or money and all parties go away satisfied and happy with the transaction.

What Is Acting Responsibly?

There are many definitions of responsibility. I will list a few with examples.

Acting responsibly is:

- *Doing what you believe is right even if no one is watching.* For example, you are walking down the street, see a discarded fast-food bag, and carry it to a trash can. No one was watching you; you could have just walked by and ignored the discarded garbage.

- *Doing what you believe is right even though you won't get credit for it.* For example, you are a student and take the time to help a foreign student who is having trouble finishing as assignment because of his not having mastered English. Unless the foreign student tells someone you helped him, you will not get credit for your kindness.

- *Doing what you believe is right even though you are under pressure by peers to do something that you believe to be wrong.* For example, you are a teenager who is out with his buddies late at night. They decide it would be "fun" to throw rocks at the house of an elderly couple to scare them out of their sleep. You are the only one in the group who disagrees with the idea. You try to talk them out of it even though they make fun of you and berate you.

- *Doing what you believe is virtuous even though it may be against the law.* Obeying legitimate laws is an obvious act of responsibility. However, what do you do if you think the legitimate law is unjust and is doing harm? For example, people under German laws or edicts in the Second World War helped Jews who were supposed to be turned in to the authorities. In violation of the laws and at great jeopardy to themselves, they hid Jews and helped them escape. They broke the law because they had a higher ethical standard than the lawmakers.

- *Fulfilling your needs without hindering or depriving others of fulfilling their needs.* For example, I am aware of an unfortunate business (Ponzi scheme) where a man and wife bilked investors out of many millions of dollars. Many of the investors were elderly and in ill health. Some invested their total life savings into the business. When the business finally went bankrupt, it was discovered that the ill-gotten gains had been used by the business owners to buy opulent houses, expensive jewelry, fancy cars, and other conspicuous signs of consumption. They irresponsibly fulfilled their wants while depriving others of their needs. A responsible business owner would conduct her business to make a profit to meet her needs and wants, and to continue the enterprise. She would also build into her business model such things as fair and adequate salaries that can help employees gain financial security, a work environment that promotes physical and mental health, and opportunities for employees to advance in the company based on their skills and work ethics. I personally think that a good CEO would also look at the disparity between her and employees' take-home pay. Is the disparity fair? Is it responsible to have huge disparities? Just asking.

- *Taking full and ultimate personal responsibility for your actions.* You take full and ultimate responsibility for the decisions you make about your physical health and mental health. You take total responsibility for the decisions that are made about your finances, even if you have a financial advisor. You are ultimately responsible for continuing to learn new skills that make you a better problem-solver and critical thinker. You are totally responsible for how you treat other people, the environment, and yourself.

Given the above discussion and nuances about the definition, the definition we can use here is, "Acting responsibly is fulfilling my needs without hindering or depriving others of fulfilling their needs." I have not included both *needs* and *wants* here as I have done in other economic discussions in the book. I deliberately did not include *wants* because they are not necessary. They are often short-term fun but not necessary to life, happiness or fulfillment. For example, many wealthy people have long ago fulfilled their *needs* and everything after that is only a *want*. Poor people might not even have basic needs met. Hence, those who greedily continue to gather personal wealth—long after they have fulfilled their needs and purchased every want possible—yet still pay employees below living wages are acting both irresponsibly and immorally using this definition.

Responsibility to Others

Acting responsibly to others is a necessary practice if a society is to smoothly function and perpetuate itself. If we all act responsibly to one another, we will have no crime, we won't need police, we needn't fear that agreements will be broken, and we will all be happier and more productive individually and as a society. We are acting responsibly when we fulfill our needs in ways that do not hinder others from fulfilling their needs.

Some people would explain this by using the term "enlightened self-interest." This is an idea based on the understanding that what I do to enhance the quality of another's life also enhances my life. If enough people act in this way, the effect is an enhancement of the quality of life of the larger group. A less academic way of saying this is, "What goes around comes around." Others call it the boomerang theory. The way I treat others will influence how they treat me and might influence how they treat others other than me. I do not treat others responsibly in order to get an equal, in-kind favor back. I act responsibly because I think it is the "right" thing to do. If others then treat me equally responsibly, that is a positive byproduct. If the other person then goes on and practices this treating-others-responsibly habit to others in our group, it is even better.

For example, a professor named Bob, a colleague of mine at the University of Missouri, was a delightful person to be around. Many times we ate or shopped together. Every situation was the same. Bob would engage the waitress, salesperson, shopkeeper, custodian, or bus person in conversation, banter, spontaneous jokes, and other friendly chit-chat that made the occasion a pleasant one. Everyone came away from those economic transactions feeling better. There is no way to know for sure how much of

Bob's gregariousness was passed on, but I bet it was substantial. I know for sure that I try to be like Bob in similar situations and that it makes me feel good. Good things can be contagious.

Before I list some examples of responsible behaviors to others, I want to discuss another set of behaviors that I think is important and has been a source of personal good feelings and satisfaction. It is often referred to as "random acts of kindness." This is when you do something for someone for no other reason than that you want to. It is often spontaneous and is just because you want to make someone happy. For example, I was in the airport in Shanghai, China, waiting for the plane back to the United States. I noticed that I had some yuan that I had not spent. It was not enough to change back to dollars but it was enough that I didn't want to have it go to waste sitting in a drawer at home. When I was in the restroom, I noticed the attendant. He was an older man, dressed in near rags, wearing a belt that must have been several generations old. He looked physically tired and worn. I put all the money into an envelope and added a business card in case he was questioned about where he got the money. When I gave him the envelope, he went into a stall to see what it was. I left, expecting to never see him again. However, the plane was late and I had to use the restroom again. When the attendant recognized me, he gave me a look that I will never forget. Although in quite different ways, we were both much happier. Especially me.

Here is a short sample of responsible actions toward others:

- Treat everyone with respect, especially those whom society tends to look down upon.

- Treat others as if they have no limits to their potential. People can accomplish just about anything if they want to badly enough and are willing to spend the time.

- One of the best things you can do for other people is to help them become more self-reliant. This is especially true for those who have been marginalized in our society.

- Understand that your decisions will have consequences to others as well as yourself. You need to determine who might be impacted by your actions and whether those consequences will be positive or negative for them. Try to identify unintended consequences before they occur.

- When negotiating with others, suppress the competitive urge to win everything overwhelmingly. Seek win-win outcomes that satisfy everyone as much as possible.

- Follow through on your promises.

- Don't be greedy in your economic transactions. Pay what something is worth.

- Teach youths at an early age, especially boys, that if they parent a child they are morally responsible to provide for that child until he or she becomes an adult.

- Avoid physical confrontations.

- Deal with others as individuals. It is almost always less helpful to think of individuals as members of an "ethnic group" or "race." Those terms and others like them are outmoded categorizations that only muddle thinking because they encourage overgeneralizations and stereotyping.

- Do not gossip.

- Of course, do not use derogatory names or categorizations of other humans.

- Be a model of the five factors in this book to show others how they might make their lives. You don't have to say anything—just be a model.

- Do not bully or allow others to bully.

- Work for and vote for public officials who demonstrate (promising doesn't count) that they are responsible representatives of their constituencies and are promoting some of this book's five factors.

- Rule out cheating unless it is when you are playing solitaire.

- Don't drive if you have been drinking or taking any drug that might impair you, even if it is prescribed by a doctor.

- If someone offends you in some way, instead of judging him as stupid, inconsiderate or bad, choose to act on the premise that "He did the best he could with his knowledge and understanding at the time under the circumstances as he saw them." Try this approach and see how it works for you.

- Make it a habit to try to add value to relationships and encounters with others.

- Consider going out of your way to do "something nice" for someone whom you don't like or who you think doesn't like you.

- Celebrate the differences in us humans and learn from them.

- In relating to others, remember that nobody wants to be told what to do.

- Look upon others as "just different," not superior or inferior.

Be aware of others and their needs as much as possible. Practice empathy.

Responsibility to the Environment

Our planet, our home, is finite. It has been compared to a spaceship. Both provide their passengers with all the things we need to stay alive, but those resources can be exhausted. The spaceship has an obvious limited amount of oxygen, water, food, and other provisions which the astronauts are trained to conserve and recycle. Earth is the same although we don't often pause to think about the limitations. Our planet also has limited resources to sustain us, but we earthlings for the most part are not trained or even aware of the need to nurture these resources. Most of us simply take our environments for granted and as something to exploit for short-term gains without considering the long-term consequences of that exploitation.

We live on a finite planet, but we humans put infinite demands on it. Worldwide we breed and multiply our human population with little voluntary control. We usually define *development* as making and consuming more of just about everything, which leads to us demanding increasing amounts of resources to make and use all the *stuff*. For example, automobile manufacturers strive to sell as many cars and trucks as they can. They want to create and then meet a worldwide demand for more vehicles. Few people question this quest to sell infinite numbers of vehicles. It is understandably difficult for an organization whose survival is based on consumption of its products to have voluntary self-restraint in the amount of product it produces. Much of this problem is from what I will call "blind consumption."

We who live in the United States have been the leaders in "blind consumption." The vast majority of us seem to operate on ideas like "more is better," "bigger is better," "faster is better," "newer is better," "easier is better," "prestige brands are better," and "expensive is better." We have been taught these ideas by the acceptance of mass advertising. Schools and parents do not teach children critical-thinking skills like propaganda analysis and logical fallacies, so we have little defense against being brainwashed and becoming world-champion practitioners of blind consumption.

For example, the United States, with only about 5 percent of the world population, consumes about 25 percent of the world's coal, oil, and natural gas. Another example: As early as 2003, Americans owned more private automobiles that there were licensed drivers. Also, from 1975 to 2003, American homes increased in average size by nearly 40 percent while at the same time the average number of people per house decreased. Look around at the sizes of homes and vehicles today. Count the electronic gadgets we now think we need. All of this is having a huge impact on our environment. And the rest of the world wants to be just like us.

I have had the opportunity to live and travel in much of the world in such a way that I can observe and interact with a cross section of people in those countries. Almost every person admires the American lifestyle, strives to be like Americans, and tries to imitate American ways of life as best he or she can. Their dreams include fancy cars, designer clothes, bigger houses, the newest in electronics, sugary drinks, lots of added meat in their diets, snack foods, American TV shows, American movies and music, and the Internet, of course. We have set the benchmark for "happiness" in the eyes of much of the world. (As an aside, I have observed that as groups of people have adopted our lifestyles, they have become more obese, less healthy, and no happier. Their ideal when adopted has become their ordeal.) The obvious point here is that if the most admired lifestyle in the world is based on unrealistic consumption of finite resources, what will happen as more and more people also adopt this lifestyle? What will happen when China and India behave like we Americans do? Add South America and Africa to those emulating the lifestyle we enjoy. Look out, Mother Earth!

What Can You and I Do?

As I have pondered and researched what we might do to help slow down (probably can't completely stop) the degrading of our immediate environment and the planet as a whole, I have found thousands of suggestions. I will list some below. Just as we have been the model of "blind consumption," maybe we can now be the model of a reformed consumption addict and demonstrate to the world that we have learned some valuable lessons. We can be models of "informed consumption" and the use of common sense in the way we treat our environment. Note also that these suggestions almost always will save you money and be advantageous to you personally as well as take some pressure off our environment.

Here is a selection of suggestions for what you and I can do that go beyond the obvious and most often repeated:

- **Repair broken items if possible.** If they are not repairable, then recycle and replace them.

- **Replace grass with something that grows naturally in your part of the country.** Grass requires fertilizer that washes into our streams and drinking water. Grass needs water that is becoming increasingly scarce in many places. It needs cutting, which requires machinery that is often a source of pollution. Grass needs to be disposed of, which takes energy for hauling. It is expensive for a homeowner both monetarily and in terms of time. Grass started being used by the elite to show their status and has become a habit with many people because "I just like it. It looks pretty." To those of us who have studied the matter, "it just looks stupid." Especially to those of us who live in the desert.

- **Treat public property such as parks, roadways, reserves and other common areas as if you owned them ... because you do.**

- **Buy your food as local as possible.** It will be fresher for you, will save transportation, and will keep local jobs.

- **Have an energy audit done of your home.** This will provide ideas of what needs to be done to make your home more energy-efficient and how much that will cost. Then, depending on what you can afford, do those items that are the most efficient.

- **Eat more plant-based foods.** Not only are they more nutrient-rich than animal-based foods, they are also less detrimental to the environment. For example, it takes about 2,500 gallons of water to raise one pound of beef. It also takes about twelve pounds of grain, thirty-five pounds of topsoil and the energy of about one gallon of petroleum. That is for one pound of beef. That's only the start. Take some time to look it up.

- **Consider having fewer or no children.** The world is overpopulated now, and it is getting rapidly worse. If you don't think you want to help the overpopulation problem, do it for your own selfish sake. You will have more time and money for yourself and your family for each child you do not have. There is probably no problem in the world that wouldn't be helped if there were fewer humans.

- **Participate in organizations that are trying to lessen the problems of overpopulation.** Even though it would be doomed, suggest to your representative in

Congress that there should be a tax for each child, not a tax deduction.

- **Participate in recycling programs with your municipality.** Many stores will recycle plastic bags for you. Recycle discarded clothing, appliances, furniture, and other household items with organizations that will sell them to support worthy organizations and the people who work there.

- **Go online to find lists of things you can do to conserve our environment.** There are thousands of conservation ideas not only about everyday living but also about starting businesses. Most of the ideas will also save you money.

- **Consider getting your recreation using human-propelled, nonmotorized "toys" such as bicycles, skis, canoes, kayaks, sailboats, and hiking boots.** These are cheaper and they don't harm the environment— and you will get some exercise, which most of us could use more of. In addition to our transportation vehicles for family and work, many of us have several motorized "toys" such as motorboats, motorcycles, Jet Skis, snowmobiles, pontoon boats, ATVs, dune buggies, and other recreational conveyances. These usually pollute more than automobiles do. Depending on the recreational vehicle and where it is used, it can pollute the water and air, cause erosion and destroy vegetation, scare animals, disturb people seeking peace and quiet, cause accidents, and use lots of gas.

- **Consider downsizing if you haven't already done so.** In almost every case, smaller means less impact on the environment and less impact on your wallet. For example, I once had an employee (married with no children) who drove to work (long commute) in a huge SUV. When she was complaining how much it was costing her in gas, insurance, loan payments, taxes, and other maintenance, I asked her why she drove such a big vehicle. She explained that once a year her family got together for a long week and she needed the large vehicle to haul all of them during their stay. She had not considered buying a smaller, cheaper, less-costly car for her commuting during the year and then simply renting a van for the one week of hauling her family. When we compared the costs, the difference was huge, and she disclosed that she hated driving and especially parking the large SUV.

I know many people do the same thing with their home purchases. They purchase a home big enough to accommodate the largest number of people who might visit at the same time. As a result they purchase a home that is more expensive to purchase and maintain, has higher insurance and taxes, has higher utility bills, and is harder to keep clean. All of these extra costs could be saved by purchasing a smaller home and in the event of overflow purchasing people a nice hotel room. You would be surprised how many people would choose the peace and quiet of a hotel room for the evening if given the chance.

- **Your yard is the next place you might want to downsize if you get the opportunity.** We Americans still perpetuate the farmer's need for lots of land. Big yards are usually seen as an asset to home purchasers. It is not that we need the extra space, it is that we are still programmed to desire it. Most American homes are lessons in wasting land. Most houses have large, ornamental front lawns—usually grass, some trees, and some shrubs. They are not usually used by the families who own them. It is usually not desirable for neighbor children or pets to utilize them. They are for ornamentation, to look nice and impress those who pass by. They are expensive to maintain and require much of the discretionary time of an occupant of each home to do upkeep. We usually have side yards that take up space but are also not used except for being an occasional passageway. Backyards are usually to be used by children and pets for play and by adults for entertaining. They should be the largest part of our yards, because we use them the most. If you are going to build or purchase a new home, look for one that minimizes the size of the yards that are not used and maximizes the yard areas that are most used. You might start by looking for zero-lot-line house placements. Of course, the best solution is to live in a high-rise that has common areas for recreation and entertainment.

- **Be careful what you flush down the toilet.** It is not an appliance that magically disposes of any waste without harm to the environment, even though it is often treated that way. Use it only for what it was designed to do.

- **Simply buy less stuff.** Most of us have closets, garages, basements, attics, sheds, and even rented storage spaces where we store stuff we do not use. It costs the environment to make this stuff and it will cost the environment when we dispose of it. We don't have to buy most of the stuff in the first place. One theory is that we are forced to buy all this stuff in order to fill up our great big oversized houses.

- **Live as simply as possible.** I take this to mean fulfilling our basic human needs and going easy on all the wants that we are encouraged by advertising to obtain. For example, I purchase the most nutritious food possible without consideration of the cost because it is a basic need. However, I am very conscious of the monetary and environmental costs of things I simply want.

- **Plant lots and lots of trees.** Trees "breathe" in carbon dioxide and "breathe" out oxygen. What better way to renew our air?

- **Consider water (and air) as being owned by everybody.** I can't believe it when I still see people leave the water running in the sink during the total time they shave or brush their teeth, or even when they are arranging their hair. Wasting water in the gym, hotel, public bathroom, or anywhere that is not your home is still wasting water.

- **Use as few insecticides, herbicides, and other chemical "killers" as possible.** Try to think of the *unintended consequences* of using any chemicals when you are tempted to do so.

- **Report things or events that you think are harming the environment to the local authorities.** This would be things like illegal dumping, water leaks, or water being misused, natural gas leaks, diseased plants, and illegal burning.

- **Become aware of the environmental issues in your area and take part in governmental discussions and decisions.** Maybe run for an office or volunteer to serve on a board. These environmental issues, if not resolved, not only can lead to health problems but can also lead to decreased property values and other financial problems for you and your municipality.

I must point out, perhaps at the risk of life and limb, that our fascinations, love, and sometimes addictions for having pets are also a problem for the environment. Studies suggest that pets can have positive impacts on humans' blood pressure, depression, anxieties and other stress-related symptoms. That's why we love pets. They make us feel good. They are often treated as members of the family and as if they were another child. In fact, some animals are treated better than children.

The point is that pets, especially the large ones, can be expensive for a family to maintain, and they have a negative impact on the environment just as humans do. Human overpopulation is a larger problem by far, but a little research can bring out the specific problems and possible solutions associated with having pets. A few quick facts are that over 60 percent of households in America have pets. The most popular pets are dogs and cats. Dogs and cats are carnivores. Producing animal-based food is damaging to the environment whether it is for pets or humans. A different estimate is that a large dog has about as much negative impact on the environment as a human child.

Another estimate was that a medium-size dog does about as much damage to the environment as a Toyota Land Cruiser with a 4.6-liter engine that is driven 10,000 miles. Another article estimated that more than half of the deaths of birds are caused by "outside cats" and feral cats. There is a large amount of research being done on the amount of environmental damage done by the pets we keep.

Much of what I read, such as the different kinds of cat litter and the problems of their disposal, was completely new to me. If you can objectively read the research, it is clear that pets have negative impacts on the environment. Whether that causes you to reduce the number or kind of pets you have (goldfish seem to be least problematic) is obviously up to you. There are a huge number of variables both pro and con to having pets. At least look into it; whatever direction you choose, you will find it interesting. I am simply the messenger of questions and information ... please, pet lovers, do not try to kill the messenger.

The environment has been here long before you and me. It will be here long after you and I are gone. The environment doesn't care about humans. It will adjust and go merrily along with or without us and those who follow us. Would it be asking too much for you and me to give some assistance to the future environment, our descendants, and all the current living things by acting with more intelligence and caring toward them than we are currently doing?

Responsibility to Yourself

This might be a little difficult to explain. When you are being responsible to yourself, you are putting yourself first in your list of priorities. The best and most-cited example is when the airline cabin attendants tell parents that in case of a lack of oxygen, oxygen masks will drop down in each seat. The parent is instructed to put his or her own oxygen mask on first and then assist the children with putting on their masks. The parent is initially responsible to herself first in order to be able to be responsible to others. So, if you want to be the best parent possible, doesn't it make sense for you to be as physically and mentally healthy as possible? Can't you be a better parent if you are financially secure and are relieved of the stress and anxiety that accompany financial insecurity? Doesn't it make sense for you to acquire a large variety of problem-solving and critical-thinking skills that you can model and teach to your children? Don't you want your children to see a parent who takes other people and the environment into consideration as a matter of everyday living and decision-making? And finally, shouldn't you as a parent be a model of self-confidence, self-esteem, and self-reliance? Shouldn't you be one of the people on the plane who has already figured out that the oxygen mask goes on you first, without the flight attendants telling you?

I know you are probably thinking that if you put yourself first, you are being selfish. *You are not being selfish, you are being smart.* Selfish people are concerned exclusively with themselves while disregarding the concerns of others.

Responsible people put themselves first in order to get their lives in such good order that they can be excellent models and teachers of others. They strive to make their lives as healthy, prosperous, intelligent, and ethical as they can—and that will better enable them to have a positive impact on others and the environment.

In the best of all worlds, you would have been taught the intricacies of the five factors by your parents, relatives, schools, churches, mass media, private and public agencies, writers, and friends. Ideally, by the time you were ready to "start on your own," you would have understood, mastered, and been successfully practicing the five factors. Your society would and should have provided you with the models and schooling to allow and encourage you to be responsible to and for yourself. The major goal of a society should be to make its youth self-reliant. As a self-reliant person, you are then capable of helping others to be self-reliant.

Here are some ideas that you might try as you act increasingly responsible to yourself:

- *Realize you can't be all things to all people all the time.* Not heeding this idea is a recipe for frustration, burnout, and poor mental health. This is true whether you are a parent, employee, boss, supervisor, or just about anybody who works with other people. It is especially important for single parents to understand.

- *Learn to politely say "no."* Busy and successful people are often asked to do more, often as volunteers. When the task does not interest you, would distract you from more important tasks, or is just something you don't want to do, politely say that you are flattered for the invitation but you will have to decline. You don't need to give any reasons. If you are asked for a reason (which is not a very tactful thing to do), give the honest one. Making up a reason on the spot that is a lie has a nasty habit of coming back to haunt and embarrass you.

- *Don't let others make their problems your problems.* This simply takes your time away from dealing with your problems. This is exemplified by the parent who, upon hearing her child complain of a problem, will consistently rush to solve the problem while the child wanders off to watch the television or play a video game. The child learns nothing about solving problems other than it is easier to get someone else to do the work. At least tell the people with the problems to try to solve the problem themselves and then come back to tell you what they think they should do, and you will give an opinion. Perhaps better, if you choose to take the time, would be to help them apply a problem-solving skill to come up with a fact-based solution. This is a prevalent issue in schools, businesses, families, and for-profit and nonprofit organizations.

- *Learn to accept praise.* If someone gives you a compliment, accept it. Say something like, "Thank you. I appreciate that." Accepting praise is a good way to add to your self-esteem. Think of self-esteem as chips you bring to a poker table. The more chips you bring to the table, the more relaxed you are. More chips, more confidence. You know you can lose a few hands and still survive. You also know if you see a really good opportunity, you can raise the stakes in the game. Translate that to your life and you can see that your self-esteem can either help you to move ahead further and faster if you have enough of it, or it can hinder your progress if you don't have enough of it.

- *Understand and use self-image.* You have thousands of self-images. We all do. For example, you have self-images of your physical attractiveness, your ability as a cook, your physical strength, your prowess as a tennis player, your open-mindedness to beliefs that are in conflict with yours, your comfort in speaking to large groups of people, your ability to change a really stinky diaper, your attributes as a poet, and your proficiency as a chicken plucker. All of these and thousands more of your self-images determine, as is stated above, your overall self-esteem. But your individual self-images are just as important or more important than the overall self-image we call self-esteem. It is the individual self-concept that can determine your initial reaction to a situation. For example, if you are a young person graduating from high school and you have no ideas of what higher education is, you probably won't even consider any further education. If you have no college graduate role models, no encouragement to further your education, and no experience with people who value further education, you probably won't even consider it. You simply don't see yourself going to college. On the other hand, if you know and admire successful college graduates and they encourage you to attend college or some other form of higher education, if your parents and the school counselor are confident that you can be successful in further education, and if you have read that college graduates make more money on the average and have more opportunities than people who don't go, you are more likely to attend some form of higher education. What you can see yourself as is what you are more likely to become.

- *Learn to analyze criticism.* First, if someone criticizes you, make sure that you understand the criticism. Your next step is to ask yourself if it is true. If you determine that it is, ask the person what he or she would do to make the situation better. I say this because the only way someone

144

can criticize you would be if he or she had something better in mind. You then thank them for the criticism and plan how you will change. Your change might incorporate the solution offered by the person who criticized you, but you make the final decision. If you determine that the criticism of you is not valid, you simply reject it and continue on your way. You might find that the criticism has some truth to it. In that case you might want to make a modification in your behavior although you wouldn't need to make a major change. The point here is that you are in control of your life and you make the decisions about the validity of criticism and your need to change.

- *Think of your potential as limitless until it is proven otherwise. That is also the way we should treat others.* Treat everybody as if they had unlimited potential until they prove otherwise. However, we are talking about you here. If you think of yourself as having unlimited potential, you are more likely to try things that you wouldn't try otherwise. Although you might not have tried something before, you are willing to try it because, with unlimited potential, you might find it to be something that you can understand, master, and enjoy. For example, you might read about nature photography in *National Geographic* magazine. Your only camera is on your smartphone, but you investigate further because you have no visual limits on what you can do. After much research, saving and planning, you find yourself on the Serengeti Plain in Tanzania, stalking animals with your new camera with long-range lenses, having the adventure of your life. Without the self-concept of unlimited potential, you might still be at home taking selfies of you and your pet chicken. The most powerful limit we put on ourselves is how we think about ourselves. Thinking of yourself as having unlimited potential allows you to explore life and uncover talents that you wouldn't discover otherwise.

- *You can learn just about anything if you want to strongly enough and you are willing to spend the time.* If you want to learn rocket science, you can do it. I am convinced that you

145

and even I can learn to be rocket scientists if we have the motivation to stick with it and are willing to stick with it for as long as it takes. The same would be true of learning to be a brain surgeon and other highly education-intensive and technical areas. Note that this concept applies to the *learning* of an area of study. You might have more limits in practice because there might be physical requirements that you could not meet even though you knew how to do them. So much is doable if we just believe more in ourselves and are willing to spend the effort.

• *Being responsible to yourself means keeping negatives out of your life as much as possible.* To help maintain your mental health, you should deliberately eliminate negative ideas, news, and people from your life. For example, there are currently some well-known radio talk show hosts who make a living "exposing" all sorts of plots, conspiracies, and other scary catastrophes they say are about to happen to us. These are almost exclusively based on rumors, hearsay, extreme radical philosophies, malicious gossip, and just plain fiction. The shows are very intense and cover a variety of topics that are unrelentingly negative. A listener, especially a frequent listener, can internalize the negativity and come to the conclusion that we, our country, our government, and the world are hopelessly doomed ... and that it's getting worse. The world can seem like a place where no one can be trusted, everything is against you, and the future is dismal and foreboding. This can lead to feelings of worry, distrust, pessimism, stress and even paranoia. This is hardly the state of mind you want to be in if you want to develop yourself into a positive, enthusiastic, realistic, optimistic leader.

Other sources of negativity are television news programs that usually stress "bad" news; commercials that are most often trying to sell you something that will cure or improve some "deficiency" or inadequacy you have with such things as your appearance, digestive tract, or bodily odors. There are also "entertainment" programs

146

and movies that are based on violence, revenge, deceit, drugs, stereotypes, and killing as the ultimate solution to conflicts. Negatives can also be internalized from friends, colleagues, music, newspapers, magazines, unpleasant (to you) surroundings, clutter and messiness, noise, "unfinished business," and held grudges.

Many people get pets that they enjoy for a while but then lose interest in. Then the animal can become a source of resentment and stress as the owner calculates the time and money to maintain it. I have been witness to overly avid sports fans (addicts?) who experience stress, anger, and other negative emotions, especially when their team is losing. Finally, it has been suggested that some of us might be negatively programming ourselves by leaving on the radio or television as we sleep. So be careful what you listen to in your bedroom while you sleep.

- *Why do you get up in the morning?* If you are like most people, you probably won't have a very clear answer. You probably haven't even given it any thought. When pushed to answer the question, you might say you get up because you need to go to work, feed the kids, or go to school. Retired people might say they get up because it is too boring to stay in bed or because they need to take a long, vigorous walk. Others might respond that they just get out of bed and figure out what to do later, just go with the flow. However, some people eagerly get out of bed and nearly always have purposeful, productive, and fulfilling days. If you don't have these kinds of purposeful days and can't clearly state why you get up in the morning, perhaps you should consider developing a personal mission statement.

A personal mission statement is a declaration that expresses your present major purpose or priority in your life. A personal mission statement gives a general direction to your life from which your more specific goals can be derived. This focus allows you to be more economical of your time, energy, and other necessary resources. For example, my current personal mission statement is "to help others to

147

gain increased control over their lives." In other words, I want to help other people to become more self-reliant, self-directed, and independent. I don't want to control others' lives, but I want them to be in control of their own lives. I believe that self-reliance should be a primary goal of parents, educational institutions, social organizations, governmental institutions, and any other organization that can influence thought and behavior. My mission statement is very compatible with my business model, research interests, writing projects, and speaking schedules. I use myself as the example, not because I want you to have a mission statement like mine, but because I can best explain the workings of my mission statement through my own experience. The development and application of my personal mission statement have made a tremendous positive difference in my personal and professional life, and I encourage you to develop your own.

Here are some other ideas about personal mission statements that should be valuable to you:

- *A personal mission statement is a broad statement of purpose that is wider in scope than a job or vocation.* It is more of a career statement in the very broadest sense.

- *Developing a personal mission statement will force you to look at your life and your purposes for living.* Your statement might be considered a rationale for your existence at this time. What is your reason for being? What are you going to do with this miracle of opportunity we call life?

- *The development of your personal mission statement will probably take some time.* It might be demanding but will certainly be intellectually stimulating. It is a process that should give you a deeper understanding of the meaning of your life.

- *Your personal statement is yours alone.* You should not seek the approval of anyone else. This is your

148

statement about what you are doing with your life. Share your statement if you desire but it is your personal declamation and doesn't need anyone else's approval.

- *Your personal mission can change.* As your life progresses, you will change, and it is likely that your mission will change, too.

- *Choose a mission in which you have strong attachments.* Have a mission statement you can express with pride and conviction. For example, I suggest that your mission statement should get a resounding YES to the question, "Will your mission, if accomplished, make the world somehow a better place?" The pursuit of more money, bigger houses, fancier cars, designer clothes, and jeweled adornments do not make good bases for personal mission statements.

- *Your mission statement should be about something you consider to be interesting, rewarding, exciting, and challenging.* It should bring out the best in you. It should take advantage of your present special interests and talents, and it should be so compelling and fascinating that you are willing to expend the energy to acquire the appropriate skills and knowledge you need but presently do not have. For example, the homemaker who has a personal mission "to promote the intellectual and physical development of my family and myself" will undoubtedly need to do extensive research to gain the knowledge and skills to achieve her mission— but it should be an exciting and valuable adventure.

- *Most mission statements deal with providing something of value to others.* These are often goods and services that people need or want. However, they often involve other living things and the environment as well as people. For example, a mission statement might deal with inventing or marketing an energy source that is economical to purchase and

149

compatible with the environment.

- *Your personal statement should benefit you as well as others.* You are not sacrificing your life for the lives of others. Ideally, you are adding value to the world in some ways and in the process are adding value to yourself. Most good personal missions, even though aimed primarily at the benefit of others, will very likely "rub off" on you, too.

A personal mission statement is a commitment to a way of life. It states what you stand for and commits you to a lifestyle that is consistent with that philosophy. This lifestyle defines you and what you are about. It gives direction and purpose to your life. It should increase the probability that your life will be more enriched, positive, and fulfilling. It should be a major reason why you want to get out of bed in the morning. Maybe even earlier than usual.

Final Thoughts

I started explaining why you should feel responsibility to yourself by giving the example of the parent and child in a plane preparing for a takeoff. The instructions in the event of a loss of oxygen are for the parent to put his or her own mask on first, then help the child with his or her mask. I really like that example, but I want to share another appropriate but different example from the late Zig Ziglar. It went like something like this:

Pretend you are the owner of a $10 million race horse. Would you feed it junk food? Would you let it stand around in a stall all day watching television, playing video games, texting other horses, eating snacks loaded with fat and salt and sugar, drinking only sugary drinks because it "just likes them," and let it stay up until late at night drinking beer and watching "reality shows?" No. If you wanted to protect your valuable investment, you would research, purchase, and feed your horse the most nutritious and healthy food possible. You would research the best training regime and exercise schedule for your horse so that it could be as healthy and fit as possible. You would research and implement the most appropriate sleep schedule for that expensive horse. You would respect it, love it, treat it with kindness, and do everything possible to optimize its potential.

I am asking you to treat yourself at least as well as you would that horse. You are more important than that horse. You have much more potential than that horse. You have so much more to give than the horse. The horse is worth $10 million. You are a priceless miracle, and you should treat yourself that way.

Key concepts and terms that you can research to further investigate acting responsibly to others, the environment and yourself:

- Myths of race and ethnicity.

- Ecology.

- The golden rule (with caveats).

- Enlightened self-interest, boomerang theory.

- "Us" versus "them."

- Labeling others and self.

- Integrity.

- Equal opportunity.

- Innocent until proven guilty.

- Ethics.

- "Doing the best he can" approach.

- The many kinds of pollution.

- Formal and informal language.

- Selective forgetting.

- Dignity.

- What behaviors and values do you model?

- Change as a constant.

- Self-reliance.

- Different, not superior or inferior.

- Discrimination, just or unjust?

- Parenting responsibilities.

- Stereotyping, overgeneralizing.

- Democracy.

- Spectator or participant?

- Population problems.

- Individual and group behaviors.

- Respect.

- Rights and responsibilities.

- Theory of the commons.

- Do no harm.

- Fairness.

- The economy versus the environment.

- Vested interests.

- Seeking balances.

- Heroes.

- Hate.

- Greed.

- Envy.

- Diplomacy.

- Conformity versus nonconformity.

- How do you treat the environment?

- Win-win negotiating.

- Nation states.

- History as interpretation.

- Is America the rich, spoiled kid on the block?

- What do you take for granted?

- What is a patriot?

- National and political myths.

- What does the U.S. model to other nations?
- Why care about the environment?
- Don't bother me with reality, entertain me.
- People versus the environment.
- In case of emergency, apply your oxygen mask first.
- Lifestyle.
- Grass as an enemy.
- War and other really stupid stuff.
- Perspective.
- Freedom.
- Compassion.
- Humor.
- Recycling.
- Buying local.

You are a miracle. Treat yourself that way.

Living Intelligently:
A Final Note and a Challenge

I use the word "intelligence" in the same way that an espionage agency uses it. A spy agency constantly gathers useful information that can be used by its country for defensive or offensive purposes. *Intelligence is useful information.* It is not some bogus guess at a person's innate capacity for thinking, as it usually is used.

Like a dedicated spy, I have worked for decades gathering and distilling the intelligence in this book for you to use to defend yourself against the uninformed and the devious who could wreck your life if you let them. There are all sorts of people who are trying to get you to do what they want you to do. They will use all sorts of mind and word tricks to get your money, your vote or your unquestioned allegiance. Most of us are content to aimlessly wander through our miracles of life unquestioningly pursuing what advertisers, politicians, preachers, teachers and our traditions tell us to buy, believe, love, hate, and die for. They don't want us to possess useful information. They want us to rely on them for our information. They count on our being uninformed (stupid?) or too complacent to care. That's why we need to be as self-reliant as possible.

I challenge you to launch a small but robust revolution to help yourself be healthier physically, mentally, and financially. I exhort you to start a personal crusade to stamp out ignorance by learning and practicing more of the many skills of problem solving and critical thinking. I implore you to seek out increasingly responsible actions to others, to the environment, and especially to yourself. This can be your personal revolution.

Trade some of the time you spend following sports, Twitter, Facebook and all the other social media, reality shows, sitcoms, music, celebrity gossip, movies, TV, fiction, and all the other forms of "recreation" for some time gathering crucial intelligence that could fundamentally and positively change your life.

You only have one life. And the question you must ask yourself is:

WHAT'S MOST IMPORTANT?